1000 FACTS
HISTORY
TIMELINES

First published by Bardfield Press in 2005
Copyright © 2005 Miles Kelly Publishing Ltd

Bardfield Press is an imprint of
Miles Kelly Publishing Ltd,
Bardfield Centre, Great Bardfield, Essex, CM7 4SL

Some material in this book appears in *Visual Factfinder History Timelines*

2 4 6 8 10 9 7 5 3 1

Editorial Director
Belinda Gallagher

Editorial Assistant
Amanda Askew

Designer
Tom Slemmings

Design
Q2A

Indexer
Jane Parker

Scanning and reprographics
Anthony Cambray, Mike Coupe, Ian Paulyn

British Library Cataloguing-in-Publication Data
A catalogue record for this book is available from the British Library

ISBN 1-84236-553-3

Printed in China

www.mileskelly.net
info@mileskelly.net

1000 FACTS
HISTORY
TIMELINES

Consultant: Rupert Matthews

BARDFIELD PRESS

Contents

Contents

Contents

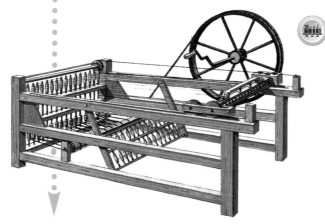

Contents

*c.***4600 million years ago** Dust and gas floating in space came together to form the Earth.

*c.***3500 million years ago** The first life forms on Earth – single-celled bacteria and blue-green algae – appeared.

*c.***500 million years ago** A variety of creatures such as shelled invertebrates, marine plants and fish appeared.

*c.***245–146 million years ago** The continents divide. Reptiles, particularly dinosaurs, dominated this period.

*c.***146–65 million years ago** Modern continents began to form. Flowering plants and mammals appeared. Dinosaurs become extinct.

*c.***65–2 million years ago** Mammals dominated the Earth.

*c.***2 million years ago** *Homo habilis* made tools for hunting; and, later, *Homo erectus* used fire to cook.

*c.***200,000 years ago** *Homo sapiens* appeared.

*c.***90,000 years ago** Fully modern humans evolved in Africa. They then spread out across the world.

▶ *The coelacanth appeared about 350 million years ago. It was thought to have become extinct some 60 million years ago, but was found again in 1938.*

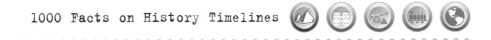

▼ *A stone-age hunter. These early people made a variety of chipped stone tools for many different purposes.*

*c.***35,000**BC Tools with handles were devised. For example, stone spearheads attached to wooden handles appeared during this time.

*c.***11,000–10,000**BC The first farmers cultivated wheat in Mesopotamia, the area between the rivers Tigris and Euphrates, in West Asia.

*c.***9000**BC Jericho, one of the earliest settlements and farming communities, was established on the western bank of the Jordan River.

8000–5000 BC

*c.*8000 BC Mesopotamians began using clay tokens of different shapes to keep accounts of land, food and livestock.

*c.*8000–6000 BC The people of Jericho made textiles from linen, which they dyed and decorated with shells.

*c.*7400–6700 BC The people of Mexico began forming agricultural communities.

*c.*7000 BC Humans reached South America. Initially they formed small groups and hunted for food.

*c.*7000–5000 BC In China, small agricultural settlements developed in which people cultivated rice.

*c.*7000–4500 BC The earliest permanent Egyptian settlements were established.

*c.*6000 BC A primitive agricultural settlement that grew wheat developed at Mehgarh, west of the Indus Valley.

*c.*6000 BC The aboriginal people of northern Australia made rock paintings of wild animal life.

*c.*5000 BC Agricultural people arrived in southern Italy by boat. They cultivated wheat, reared sheep and cows and made pottery.

*c.*5000–4000 BC In China, there were several settled cultures with distinct artistic styles.

...FASCINATING FACT...
The world's oldest bakery was discovered at the pyramid workers' village at Giza. It was tall, cylindrical and had a conical top. The firebox was at the bottom and there were shelves inside for cooking the dough.

▼ *An ancient Chinese village.*
Animals such as pigs, dogs
and cattle were domesticated
in China around 5000BC.

4000–2950BC

*c.*4000BC Egyptians discovered weaving and dyeing, and began making clothes.

*c.*4000BC People from Turkey migrated to Sumer, south of Mesopotamia. They farmed, traded and developed a number of crafts. These Sumerians later invented cuneiform writing, the ox-drawn plough and wheel.

*c.*3600BC A primitive form of writing was developed in Mesopotamia.

*c.*3500BC Independent city-states gained power in various parts of Mesopotamia.

*c.*3500BC The Chinese studied cracks on heated ox bones and turtle shells to tell the future. Jade was used widely in making figurines and jewellery.

*c.*3500BC In the Indus Valley, ceramics, copper artefacts and carved seals were decorated with abstract patterns.

*c.*3200BC Settlements around the Aegean Sea flourished. The people of these areas cultivated olives, grapes and cereals. Metalwork was widespread.

*c.*3100BC In Britain, the first stage of building Stonehenge began.

*c.*3000BC The Minoan civilization emerged in Crete. It was one of the earliest great civilizations of the world.

◀ *The invention of the wheel was one of the most important landmarks of human civilization. By 3200BC the Sumerians had built four-wheeled carts like the one shown here.*

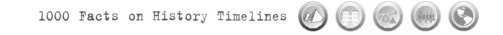

▲ *The builders of Stonehenge transported and erected massive blocks of stone.*

***c.*3000BC** Maize was grown in an area that is now Belize in Central America, and cotton was woven to make clothes.

***c.*2950–2575BC** The Egyptian calendar was invented. It was the first known calendar and had 365 days in a year, divided into 12 months of 30 days. The extra five or six days were added at the end of the year and were not part of any month.

2640–2000BC

*c.***2640**BC Silk was manufactured in China. In the beginning it served as a writing surface.

*c.***2630**BC In Egypt, the Old Kingdom pharaoh Djoser built the first pyramid, the Step Pyramid, at Saqqrāh in Memphis. Djoser's chief minister Imhotep was its architect.

*c.***2551–2528**BC Khufu built the Great Pyramid at Giza, Egypt. It is the largest pyramid and was considered in ancient times to be one of the Seven Wonders of the World.

*c.***2334–2279**BC Sargon, one of the earliest conquerors in world history, ruled Mesopotamia. He founded the Akkad dynasty and brought parts of Syria, Turkey and western Iran under his control. Sargon was the first leader to organize a formal military force.

▼ *The Great Pyramid at Giza, Egypt, is a major tourist attraction.*

*c.***2200–500**BC Ziggurats were built by the Sumerians in various parts of Mesopotamia. These mud brick temples were large and rectangular or square in shape.

*c.***2200**BC Egypt was weakened by crop failure and social upheavals, which led to the decline of the Old Kingdom, followed by a period of disorder, when Egypt split into several parts.

*c.***2040**BC The pharaoh Nebhepetre-Mentuhotep reunited Egypt and founded the XIth dynasty. He made Thebes his capital and his reign marked the beginning of the Middle Kingdom, which lasted until 1640BC.

*c.***2000**BC The Indus Valley civilization declined.

*c.***2000**BC The Mesoamerican Olmec civilization developed. The civilization flourished in the lowland gulf coast of southern Mexico.

*c.***2000**BC Metal began to be widely used in Egypt and Mesopotamia. Household objects such as knives, bells, weapons and jewellery were crafted out of metal.

...FASCINATING FACT...

The Indus Valley civilization was probably the first to have an advanced plumbing system. The Indus people had two-storey brick houses with a central courtyard, living rooms and bathrooms. Each house had its own well, and clay pipes below the houses carried waste to sewers that ran beneath the streets.

1792–1400BC

c.1792–1750BC Hammurabi ruled during this period in Babylon, Mesopotamia. He laid down the first known code of laws regarding acceptable social behaviour, duties of citizens and crime and punishment.

c.1766BC The Shang dynasty came to power in northeast and north central China. Remarkable bronze vessels were produced during this period for storing wine and food.

c.1630–1531BC Hyksos, people of mixed Semitic-Asian origin, conquered and ruled Egypt.

c.1600BC The Minoan civilization reached its peak on Crete. The Minoans built great palaces decorated with colourful and delicate paintings, and made elaborate earthenware.

▼ *An Egyptian charioteer driving into battle against the Hyksos. The word Hyksos is derived from the Egyptian phrase* Heka-khasut, *which means 'rulers of foreign lands'.*

◀ *A Minoan mask. The Minoan civilization was named after King Minos who, according to Greek mythology, kept a half-bull, half-human monster called the Minotaur in his palace.*

*c.*1600BC Aryans, nomadic warriors, invaded north India and drove the Dravidians, the original inhabitants, further south.

*c.*1550BC Pharaoh Ahmose I defeated the Hyksos and took over Egypt and Nubia, which was to the south of Egypt. During his reign the country prospered.

*c.*1500BC The kingdom of Kush was established to the south of Egypt.

*c.*1500BC The Mayans of Central America began making pottery utensils.

*c.*1500–1100BC The Mayans developed terraced farming to grow corn in northeastern Mexico.

*c.*1472–1458BC Queen Hatshepsut ruled Egypt. A powerful ruler, she often wore a beard and dressed like a man.

*c.*1400BC In the Soconusco region, along the Pacific coast of Guatemala, the dead were buried ceremonially and ceramic figurines, stone bowls and jewellery were placed in their graves.

17

1353-1100BC

c.1353–1336BC Pharaoh Amenhotep IV, also called Akhenaton, forced his subjects to give up old religious traditions and to worship the Sun god Aton.

c.1350BC The first public building in Mesoamerica, a timber structure on an earth platform, was built at the important settlement of San José Mogote in the Valley of Oaxaca.

c.1350BC The Lion Gate was made at the entrance to the fortress at Mycenae, Greece. Within the fortress was a palace, a shrine, a granary and houses for servants.

c.1336–1327BC Tutankhamun, the boy-king, ruled Egypt from Memphis. He ascended the throne at the age of nine and returned the country to its old religious traditions. His tomb in the Valley of Kings, one of the best preserved, was excavated in AD1922.

c.1258BC Rameses II of Egypt signed the oldest known peace treaty in the history of mankind. The treaty was between Egypt and the invading forces of the Hittites from Turkey.

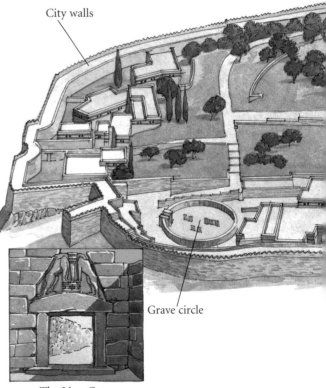

City walls

Grave circle

The Lion Gate

Store rooms
for food

Royal palace

◀ *Mycenae was one of the major centres of Greek civilization in the second millennium* BC.

Houses

*c.***1250–1200**BC The Hebrews left Egypt to settle in Palestine. They wandered in the Sinai Desert for several years, and then set about conquering Palestine.

*c.***1250**BC The city of Troy in western Turkey was sacked by an army of Mycenean Greeks.

*c.***1225**BC The Assyrians captured southern Mesopotamia and Babylon. The Assyrian state was organized for war and quickly became the centre of a large empire.

*c.***1100**BC The Indo-Aryans began using iron tools and practising Vedic religion, based on the book known today as the *Rig Veda*, written about 2000BC.

*c.***1100**BC The Dorian Greeks invaded Mycenae and the city was destroyed in a blazing fire. This marked the end of Mycenaean civilization.

1069–900BC

*c.*1069BC Egypt was in turmoil due to internal warfare and an empty royal treasury.

*c.*1045BC The Zhou dynasty replaced the Shang dynasty in China. It lasted until 256BC.

*c.*1004BC David, King of Israel, captured Jerusalem from the Jebusites and made it his capital. David united Israel and during his reign Jerusalem became an important political and religious centre.

*c.*1000–750BC This period was known as the Greek Dark Age. The Greek economy collapsed and the population declined due to constant warfare. The Greek settlements reduced in size and trade, and agriculture suffered.

*c.*1000–800BC Horse riding developed on the Eurasian steppes.

*c.*1000–450BC Small city-states developed in the southern part of Arabia. Saba was one of the oldest and most powerful among these and was a force to reckon with until AD1.

*c.*1000BC Iron became a popular metal in Europe and western Asia as people gained experience in heating, melting and forging techniques. The book of *Genesis* in the Bible mentions that Tubal-Cain was an expert ironsmith.

*c.*965BC Solomon succeeded David as the king of Israel and was famous for his wisdom and wealth. He reorganized the country into 12 administrative districts and initiated a vast building process that included the construction of the Temple of Jerusalem.

*c.*950BC In Mesoamerica, the Olmec settlement of San Lorenzo declined and La Venta gained importance. La Venta stood on an island in the Tonalá River.

*c.*900–840BC The Assyrians conquered Syria and Turkey.

▼ *The old city of Jerusalem is surrounded by massive stone walls.*

▲ *Little is known about Homer, who is regarded as the author of the epics* Iliad *and* Odyssey. *It has even been said that Homer was blind.*

c.850–480BC The Greeks learned a new technique to smelt iron ore through contact with Eastern traders. The technological innovation helped them produce better tools and weapons at a lower cost.

c.800BC In Mesoamerica, the Olmecs constructed a large earthen pyramid at La Venta. This was probably a religious structure.

c.800–700BC In Greece, the poet Homer is believed to have composed his famous epics *Iliad* and *Odyssey*. These works feature the legendary conflict between the Greeks and the city of Troy.

c.800–500BC In India, the Sanskrit texts *Brahmanas* and *Upanishads* as well as the *Sama*, *Yajur* and *Atharva vedas* were composed. These texts formed the foundation of Hinduism.

776BC The first Olympic Games were organized. The festival was thereafter held once every four years and had participants from all over the Aegean.

c.753BC According to legend, Rome was founded by the bandit chief Romulus. Romulus and his twin brother Remus were raised by a she-wolf who found them left for dead in a river.

*c.712–332*BC Egypt was invaded and ruled by the Nubians from the south, the Assyrians from northern Mesopotamia and the Persians.

*c.700*BC In Central America, the Mayans developed a written language. The script used pictures and symbols.

*c.700*BC In India, society was divided into different classes by the caste system. The *brahmins* (priestly class) were the highest caste, followed by the *kshatriyas* (warrior class). Then came the *vaishyas* (traders), followed by the *shudras* (lowest class).

*c.683*BC In many Greek city-states, monarchies gave way to republics where maintaining law and order was the responsibility of elected archons (magistrates).

▶ *The Egyptians continued to use hieroglyphs for writing on monuments long after improved writing systems were used for everyday purposes.*

23

630–540BC

*c.*630–561BC Nebuchadnezzar II reigned over Babylon. He attacked Judah and captured Jerusalem. Various projects were undertaken in Babylon during his reign, including the construction of the Hanging Gardens of Babylon.

*c.*621BC Draco, a lawmaker in Athens, set down a strict and almost tyrannical code of laws that was named after him.

*c.*600BC The religion of Zoroastrianism was founded by the prophet Zoroaster, also known as Zarathustra, in central Asia.

*c.*600BC Thespis, the Greek poet, originated the actor's role in a drama. He is considered to be the inventor of tragedy.

*c.*600BC The Mayans developed the practice of agriculture and irrigation.

They made canals to bring water to their cities in Central America. These ancient tribes mainly cultivated corn, beans and squash. The farmers used a special method to clear the jungles and also terrace the slopes of the mountains to grow crops on.

*c.*594–574BC Solon, a well-known poet, became the leader of Athens. He abolished most of Draco's harsh laws, revived the Athenian economy, minted Athenian coins and introduced weights and measures.

◀ *Nebuchadnezzar II is regarded as the greatest ruler of the Chaldean empire of Babylon.*

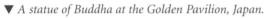

*c.***563–483**BC Buddha lived during this period, in India. He is founder of the religion Buddhism.

*c.***551–479**BC Chinese philosopher Confucius lived during this period.

*c.***545**BC The Achaemenid Empire of Persia took control of several city-states in Central Asia. The religion of Zoroastrianism spread from these cities throughout the empire.

*c.***540–520**BC The Persians conquered the Greek city-states in Asia Minor and captured Egypt.

▼ *A statue of Buddha at the Golden Pavilion, Japan.*

509–400BC

▶ *Most of what we know of Socrates comes from the writings of his students Plato and Xenophon.*

509BC King Tarquin the Proud was expelled from Rome, which then became a republic.

***c.*500BC** In present-day Nigeria, settlements were formed and people began to make iron tools.

492–449BC Greece and Persia were engaged in a series of battles, which are collectively referred to as the Greco-Persian Wars. Athens defeated invading Persians in the Battle of Marathon, and then became the most powerful state in Greece.

***c.*490–430BC** Greek sculptor Phidias lived during this period. He was the chief sculptor of the Parthenon and created the statue of Zeus for the Temple of Zeus at Olympia.

***c.*475–221BC** The Zhou dynasty in China broke up into several small warring states.

***c.*451–450BC** *The Twelve Tables of Roman Law* were the first set of laws laid down by the Roman Republic.

***c.*450–388BC** Greek playwright Aristophanes lived during this period. He wrote 40 plays including *Wasps* and *Clouds*, and is regarded as the greatest comic dramatist of ancient Greece.

◄ *Legend has it that Pheidippides ran a distance of 40 km from Marathon to Athens to convey news of the Battle of Marathon.*

c.445BC After leading the Greek cities to defeat Persia, Athens tried to enforce its own rule on other Greek states. In 431BC this led to the Peloponnesian War between Athens and Sparta. All Greek cities took sides. In 405BC, the two sides agreed to a truce. The Peloponnesian War weakened the Greek cities and ruined their economy.

c.428–348BC The Greek philosopher and teacher Plato lived during this period. He was a student and close friend of Greek philosopher Socrates.

c.400BC *Tao-te Ching,* or *Classic of the Way of Power,* was written by Lao-tzu. The Taoism religion was based on this.

. . . **FASCINATING FACT** . . .
In ancient Greece only young men from aristocratic families were educated. At the age of 18 they had to spend two years in a gymnasium, where they were prepared, physically and mentally, to enter adulthood. To study subjects such as philosophy, mathematics and logic, students had to attend Plato's Academy or Aristotle's Lyceum.

400–301BC

*c.***400BC** In southern Mexico, the Zapotecs used a 365-day solar calendar as well as a 260-day ritual calendar.

*c.***400BC** In Mesoamerica, the Olmec city of La Venta lost its importance.

384–322BC Greek philosopher Aristotle lived during this period, teaching that logic governed everything.

336BC Philip II of Macedonia was assassinated and his son Alexander the Great became king.

*c.***335BC** Aristotle founded the Lyceum school that specialized in biology and history.

331BC Alexander the Great defeated the Persians in the Battle of Gaugamela, capturing their vast empire.

323BC Alexander died in Babylon after conquering most of the known world.

▲ *A great general, Alexander is famous for overthrowing the Persian Empire.*

*c.***312BC** The Romans built the first aqueduct to bring water to Rome.

*c.***304**BC Chandragupta Maurya, King of Magadha, expanded his empire in India and founded the Maurya dynasty.

301BC The generals of the Macedonian army divided Alexander's empire between themselves.

▲ *The ancient Romans built 11 aqueducts to supply water to the capital. The longest of these could bring water to Rome from a distance of as much as 92 km.*

. . . . FASCINATING FACT. . . .
Ptolemy II, King of Egypt, founded the Library of Alexandria at the beginning of the 3rd century BC. He asked every country in the world to send copies of their books, making it the largest collection of its time.

300–180BC

c.300BC The city of Teotihuacán was established. One of the greatest Mesoamerican cities, it was situated near springs that provided water for irrigation. Obsidian, used for making tools and weapons, was also found here in large quantities.

c.294–284BC A giant bronze statue of the Sun god Helios was erected at Rhodes, Greece. The Colossus of Rhodes was 32 m high and was considered to be one of the Seven Wonders of the World. Arabian invaders destroyed it in AD653.

c.290–212BC Greek mathematician and inventor Archimedes lived during this period. He discovered the law of buoyancy, which is also known as the Archimedes principle.

264–241BC The Romans defeated the Carthaginians in the First Punic War and captured Sicily.

▶ The Colossus of Rhodes took 12 years to build. It was toppled by an earthquake in 226BC.

c.260BC Asoka succeeded his father Bindusara. One of India's most famous rulers, Asoka played an important role in spreading Buddhism throughout the country.

c.232BC In India, Emperor Asoka died and the Mauryan Empire began to crumble.

221–207BC The Qin dynasty unified all China. King Shih Huang-ti, who declared himself the first emperor of China, built the Great Wall of China. In 206BC the Qin was replaced by the Han dynasty.

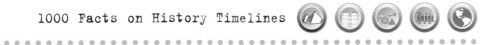

218–201BC The Second Punic War between Rome and Carthage began when Rome broke the treaty of 241BC. The Carthaginian general Hannibal led an army to Italy, where he defeated the Roman Army in 216BC. Rome refused to surrender and defeated Carthage in 202BC. Rome became the most powerful state in the Mediterranean.

*c.***200BC** In the southwest of North America, famine led to the decline of village cultures.

*c.***180BC** The last Mauryan king was killed by his commander-in-chief, Pushyamitra Sunga, who established the Sunga dynasty. The Satavahanas came to power in southern and central India.

▼ *Teotihuacán was one of the largest cities of its time. The ruins of the city contain great palaces, plazas and temples. The Pyramid of the Sun is one of the largest structures built in the ancient Americas.*

31

146BC—AD1

146BC The Romans invaded Greece and by 30BC had conquered the area.

106–43BC Cicero lived during this period. He was a great Roman orator, lawyer, scholar and writer, in favour of Rome continuing as a democratic republic.

100–44BC Julius Caesar lived during this period. He was a Roman general who rose to become dictator of the Roman Empire between 46 and 44BC.

*c.***73–71BC** Gladiators of Rome revolted against the Republic in the Gladiatorial War. Spartacus, a gladiator from Thrace, was leader of the revolt.

63BC The Romans defeated the Jews and occupied Palestine.

51BC The beautiful Cleopatra VII was made queen of Egypt by Julius Caesar. When she ascended the Egyptian throne, she was only 17 years old.

44BC Brutus, Cassius and other aristocrats in the Senate murdered Julius Caesar in an attempt to restore democracy.

31BC After a series of civil wars, Octavian, the nephew of Julius Caesar, defeated his enemies at the Battle of Actium. Among the defeated were Roman general Mark Antony and Queen Cleopatra of Egypt. Octavian assumed the title Augustus and became the first emperor of Rome. The Roman Empire included large parts of Europe and Asia, northern Africa and the Mediterranean islands.

*c.***4BC** Jesus Christ was born in the village of Bethlehem, in Judea, during the rule of King Herod.

*c.***AD1** Teotihuacán, in central Mexico, grew into a large city due to the migration of people from surrounding areas. It had a population of about 40,000.

Gladiators were men who fought in amphitheatres to entertain ancient Romans.

AD1-60

◀ *The teachings and deeds of Jesus Christ are recorded in The New Testament and form the basic principles of Christianity.*

***c*.AD1** In North America, the Cherokee tribe lived in the southern Appalachians. They settled in the region of modern-day Virginia, West Virginia, northwestern South Carolina, northern Georgia and northern Albania.

***c*.AD1–100** The Friesians, a Teutonic tribe of German-speaking Europeans, settled in the area of the modern-day Netherlands.

AD14 Tiberius succeeded Augustus Caesar as the Roman emperor. His reign was marked by revolts in Germany, Gaul and other parts of Europe. He ruled the state efficiently and carried out reforms.

***c*.AD25** Luoyang, in China, was the capital of the Eastern Han dynasty. With a population of 500,000 people, it was the most populated city of its time.

***c*.AD30** Jesus Christ was crucified on the hill of Golgotha in Jerusalem. His teachings later formed the basis of the Christian religion.

***c*.AD30–64** Saint Peter was appointed the first leader of the Christian Church. Roman Catholics regard him as the gatekeeper of heaven

AD43 The Romans conquered southern Britain and built a bridge across the Thames at a site that is now London.

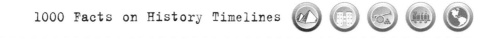

▲ *Queen Boudicca of the Iceni led a rebellion against the Romans.*

*c.*AD**45** The discovery of a shorter sea route to India by the Greeks led to the development of Calicut, in south India, into an important trading post.

AD**54–68** Roman emperor Nero ruled during this period. He was cruel to his subjects. He even had his mother, Agrippina the Younger, murdered.

AD**60** Queen Boudicca, or Boadicea, of Iceni (modern Norfolk, England) revolted against the Roman occupation of her territories. She burned London and killed 70,000 Romans before being defeated.

AD70–200

AD70 The Israelites rose in revolt against Roman rule by fighting the Jewish War, but were defeated in battle. The Romans burned the Temple of Jerusalem.

AD98 Trajan became the emperor of Rome. He expanded the empire and built several public buildings, roads and aqueducts.

*c.*AD100 Paper made from wood pulp was invented in China. Its use slowly spread across Asia and into Europe.

*c.*AD100 The Mesoamerican Olmec civilization began to decline.

*c.*AD100–200 In India, Kushan ruler Kanishka encouraged Buddhism. During this period, Buddhism spread to most parts of central Asia and China. Development of trade routes resulted in trade with Rome and Southeast Asia.

*c.*AD100–300 In Japan, farming villages grew in size. Various clans were formed, which constantly fought among themselves.

AD117–138 Roman emperor Hadrian reformed the government of the provinces. He rebuilt the Pantheon in Rome and began the construction of a large wall, known as Hadrian's Wall, in northern Britain to protect the province from the northern barbarians.

AD161–180 Marcus Aurelius ruled Rome during this period. He was a noted philosopher, and defeated several invasions during his rule.

AD177–192 The cruel and corrupt reign of Roman emperor Commodus marked the beginning of the Roman Empire's downfall.

*c.*AD200 The Bantu people, descendants of the Neolithic Nok people from west Africa, migrated into central and southern Africa.

*c.*AD200–500 Nalanda and Valabhi, important universities and centres of Mahayana Buddhism, were established in India.

▲ *Many Roman emperors built triumphal arches to commemorate their victories in battle.*

AD224-372

*c.*AD**224–641** The Iranian Sassanid dynasty ruled over Persia.

*c.*AD**250** The reign of Emperor Sujin marked the start of documented Japanese history.

AD**284–305** Roman emperor Diocletian ruled during this period. He brought peace and order after a succession of ineffective and cruel rulers.

*c.*AD**300** Armenia became the first Christian state when king, Tiridates III, made Christianity the official religion.

AD**306** Constantine the Great was made emperor by the Roman troops in Britain. He was the first Roman emperor to convert to Christianity and is widely held to be the 'first Christian emperor'.

*c.*AD**313** In Korea, the domination of the Chinese Han dynasty ended and the three Korean kingdoms of Koguryô in the north, Paekche in the southwest and Silla in the southeast, were established.

*c.*AD**317–420** Following a long period of warfare in China, the Eastern Jin dynasty brought peace and cultural development to part of the country.

*c.*AD**320** The Gupta dynasty came to power in India under the leadership of Chandragupta, a lover of art and literature. The Guptas controlled the land from the eastern hills of Afghanistan to Assam.

AD**326** Roman emperor Constantine rebuilt the ruined city of Byzantium and made it his capital. He later named the city Constantinople.

*c.*AD**372** The Huns from Central Asia drove Ostrogoths and Visigoths into Roman territory, where they were a constant source of trouble to the Romans.

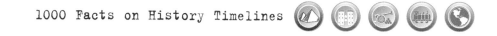

▶ *Roman emperor Constantine addresses his troops after they had made him emperor.*

◀ *The Anglo-Saxons were inhabitants of Germany who migrated to England in the 5th century and settled there.*

AD406 The Germanic tribes of Vandals, Alans and Sciri crossed the Rhine. This marked the collapse of Roman power. Four years later the Visigoths, led by Alaric, attacked and looted Rome. This was the first time Rome had been captured in 800 years.

AD434–453 Attila led the Huns. During his leadership the Huns were successful in battles against the Visigoths, Ostrogoths and the Alans.

AD476 Romulus Augustulus abdicated. He was the last Roman emperor.

c.AD476 Indian mathematician Aryabhatta devised roots and powers of numbers.

c.AD499 The Angles and the Saxons conquered what was left of Roman Britain. They established numerous small kingdoms that would later become England.

c.AD500 The city of Teotihuacán, in Mexico, covered an area of 8 sq mi and was inhibited by 150,000 people.

AD508 Frankish king, and most important king of the Merovingian dynasty, Clovis conquered most of France and Belgium, and converted all his subjects to western Catholic Christianity. Paris was made the Merovingian capital.

AD527 Justinian I ascended the Byzantine or Eastern Roman throne. He rebuilt the power of the empire.

c.AD528 Weakened by continuous invasions, the Gupta Empire in India collapsed. They were replaced by the Chalukyas who ruled over south and central India.

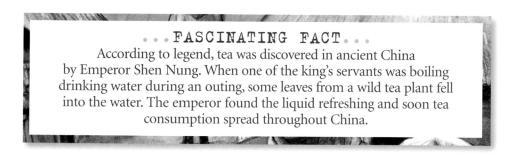

...FASCINATING FACT...

According to legend, tea was discovered in ancient China by Emperor Shen Nung. When one of the king's servants was boiling drinking water during an outing, some leaves from a wild tea plant fell into the water. The emperor found the liquid refreshing and soon tea consumption spread throughout China.

AD618-850

AD618 In China, Li Yuan established the T'ang dynasty. He united the whole of China and unified the various small kingdoms.

AD622 Opposition from Mecca's leaders forced Prophet Mohammed to flee to Medina. The event is called the *Hegira* and is considered the beginning of the Islamic era.

AD629 Dagobert I, the most powerful Merovingian ruler, united the entire Frankish land. He signed a treaty with the Byzantine emperor and campaigned against the Slavs in the east. Dagobert I shifted his capital from Austrasia to Paris. He was a patron of arts and the great abbey of Saint-Denis was built during his rule.

AD632 After the death of Prophet Muhammad, Abu Bakr became the first caliph (leader of the Islamic peoples). He was Muhammad's father-in-law as well as his trusted companion and adviser.

AD633–640 Muslim forces conquered Persia and attacked the Byzantine Empire. In Alexandria, Antioch and Jerusalem, Christian churches were turned into Muslim mosques as the lands fell to the Arab conquerors.

AD636 The Arabs defeated the Byzantines at the Battle of Yarmuk. They captured Jerusalem and destroyed the wooden cross on which Jesus Christ had been crucified.

AD661 Supporters of Ali, Muhammad's son-in-law, formed the Islamic sect called Shi'ites.

*c.***AD700** Porcelain ware was invented in China. Its name was derived from the word *porcellana*, which Marco Polo used to describe it.

*c.*AD706 Muslim invaders drove out the Zoroastrians from Persia, in modern-day Iran. The refugees travelled eastward and eventually settled in China and Gujarat, India. Zoroastrians who settled in India became known as Parsis. Those who continued to live in Persia were forced to pay a special tax to the Muslim authorities.

AD732 Frankish ruler Charles Martel defeated an Islamic invasion at the Battle of Tours in France.

AD768 Charlemagne ascended the Frankish throne and united most of western Europe. He was crowned emperor of Rome in AD800.

*c.*AD850 Several flourishing central Mexican city-states were destroyed or abandoned, probably due to internal problems or because of invasions by the Toltecs.

◀ *The Celtic cross is a traditional Christian symbol. It has a circle enclosing the point where the lines of the cross meet.*

43

AD850–985

*c.*AD850 The Viking prince Rurik conquered Kiev and established the Rus dynasty, from which the name Russia derives.

*c.*AD868–1000 The Vikings discovered and colonized Iceland, Greenland and parts of North America.

*c.*AD895 The Magyars migrated from Siberia and settled down in modern-day Hungary and parts of Romania.

*c.*AD900 The Toltecs ruled the area from Costa Rica to the southwest of North America, from Tula, their capital city.

*c.*AD906 Annam, or central Vietnam, freed itself from Chinese rule. By about AD939 all of Vietnam was free.

*c.*AD946 The areas ruled by the Islamic Abbasid Caliphate became fragmented and under the control of local rulers.

AD959 Edgar, King of Wessex, became king of England. He is considered the first king of England. Edgar's reign was peaceful and he was tolerant towards local customs.

···FASCINATING FACT···
Unlike women in other parts of the world during the Middle Ages, Viking women played an important role in society. Vikings had to pay a bride-price to the girl's father in order to marry her. While her husband was away raiding, the Viking woman managed her home and estate. Some of them served as speakers in the court and some even went to battle!

AD960 The Sung dynasty succeeded the T'ang dynasty in China. During the Sung period, education gained importance and printed books and paper became more common.

*c.***AD985** In India, the Chola Empire reached the height of its power under Rajaraja Chola. He built the famous Brihadeeswara temple in Tanjavur.

▲ *The Vikings from Scandinavia invaded vast areas in eastern and western Europe from* AD*800 to 1100.*

45

AD988–1066

AD988 Vladimir I, the grand duke of Kiev, converted to Christianity and popularized the customs of the Orthodox Church in Russia.

AD997 Mahmud of Ghazni invaded north India and conquered Punjab. He was the ruler of the Ghaznavid Empire based in Afganistan.

*c.*1000 The Cholas of south India conquered Sri Lanka.

1016–1035 Canute, Prince of Denmark, became the king of England, Denmark and Norway. He issued a new law code and was a strong supporter of the Church. His rule brought peace and prosperity to England.

1031 The Omayyad Caliphate ended with the death of Caliph Hisham III.

*c.*1044 The Mons and the Burmese established the kingdom of Pagan, or Burma, in Southeast Asia.

1046 Clement II was appointed Pope by the German king Henry III, ending a disputed succession and showing imperial power over the papacy.

1048–1131 The famous Persian poet, mathematician and astronomer Omar Khayyám lived during this period. His most popular literary work is the *Rubaiyat. Rubaiyat* was later translated into English by Edward Fitzgerald.

*c.*1050–1101 Confucianism gained popularity in China. It comprised the teachings of the 5th century philosopher Confucius.

1054 A dispute between Pope Leo IX and Michael Cerularius, the leader of the Greek Orthodox Church, led to the permanent separation of the Eastern (Orthodox) and Western (Roman) churches.

1066 William I (also known as William the Conqueror), duke of Normandy, defeated Harold II of England in the Battle of Hastings and seized power as the king of England.

▼ *William the Conqueror's victory in the Battle of Hastings in 1066 marked the beginning of Norman rule in England.*

1070-1152

◀ *A medieval knight wearing the cross of a crusader.*

***c*.1070** The Tilantongo Kingdom, a small Mixtec city-state in Oaxaca, Central America, expanded its rule over a large area.

1086 Spanish king Alfonso VI captured Toledo, the Islamic centre of science. However, his success led to the invasion by the North African Almoravid Muslims, who then defeated him at Zallaqah.

1095 Pope Urban II urged all Christians to join a crusade to fight a war against Muslims.

1096 The First Crusade was fought to protect the Byzantine Empire from the Seljuk Turks. Nearly 300,000 European Christians fought in the campaign. The First Crusade succeeded in establishing a western military state in and around Jerusalem, which lasted almost two centuries.

1099 Godfrey of Bouillon, a leader of the First Crusade, captured Jerusalem and assumed the title 'Defender of the Holy Sepulchre'. He made peace with the nearby Muslim cities and resisted an Egyptian invasion.

c.1136 Suger, Abbot of Saint-Denis, France, constructed the church of Saint-Denis in a new architectural style. This was the beginning of the Gothic style of architecture.

1145 Pope Eugene III asked the French Cistercian priest Bernard of Clairvaux to call upon all Christians to begin the Second Crusade. This was in response to the Muslim capture of Edessa. The crusade failed.

c.1150 In Cambodia, the Khmer king Suryavarman II constructed the Angkor Wat temple complex, the world's largest religious structure.

1152 Frederick I, or Frederick Barbarossa, became the king of Germany. He was also crowned emperor of the Holy Roman Empire.

1152 Henry II became the king of England. He extended his empire in northern England and western France. He reformed the court system.

▼ *The crusaders succeeded in capturing Jerusalem in the First Crusade.*

1165–1187

1165 William I, also known as William the Lion, became king of Scotland.

***c.*1170** The University of Oxford was founded in England.

1170 Thomas Becket, Archbishop of Canterbury and was murdered by knights loyal to King Henry II after a dispute over Church power in England.

***c.*1171** Some Irish chieftains accepted Henry II as king of Ireland.

1171 Kurdish soldier Saladin overthrew the ruling Fatimid dynasty and seized the Egyptian throne. He later conquered Syria, Mosul (in present-day Iraq) and Mesopotamia.

***c.*1175** The Aztecs migrated towards central Mexico and probably destroyed the Toltec centre, Tula.

1184 A new Canterbury Cathedral was begun in the Gothic style by the Frenchman William of Sens.

***c.*1185** In Japan, the shogun (general) Minamoto Yoritomo took power, reducing the emperor to a mere figurehead. He appointed feudal lords called daimsyo to rule different parts of the country with the help of warriors called samurai. The Shogun system lasted almost 700 years.

1187 Sultan Saladin defeated the Christian Crusaders at the Battle of Hattin and captured Jerusalem.

▶ *A Muslim soldier from Saladin's army. Known for his military acumen, the sultan had built up a strictly disciplined army.*

...**FASCINATING FACT**...
The English scientist, Welcher of Malvern, was the first to propose dividing the Earth's surface into degrees, minutes and seconds with lines of latitude and longitude. He devised this system in 1120, after studying a solar eclipse in 1092 and trying to calculate the time difference between England and Italy.

▶ *Canterbury Cathedral was built in many stages and dates back to the 6th century. It is one of the most splendid examples of Gothic architecture in England.*

1191–1215

1191 Richard the Lionheart of England conquered Cyprus and Acre, and defeated Saladin's army in the Battle of Arsuf in Palestine. Saladin then allowed the Christians to keep the coastal towns and to travel freely to Jerusalem.

c.1200 In North America, the Cahokia tribe from the area that is now Illinois built a city with large earthen mounds used for religious purposes.

c.1200 Cuzco, in Peru, developed into an important Inca centre. It was also known as 'City of the Sun'. It was regarded as sacred to the Sun god.

c.1201 Venice became an important commercial centre in Europe under the rule of an elected ruler called the Doge.

1202 Pope Innocent III called for the Fourth Crusade. Instead of attacking the Moslems, the Crusaders quarrelled with the Christian Byzantine Empire and captured Constantinople.

1206 Mongol ruler Genghis Khan united the nomadic Mongol tribes of Central Asia. He attacked China and by 1215 had captured Beijing and overthrown the Sung dynasty.

> ...FASCINATING FACT...
> The 13th-century Indian poet-saint Gyandev devised a game played with cowrie shells and dice, in which players moved up ladders (representing 'good') or were eaten by snakes (representing 'evil'). The game is still popular and is known by the name of 'snakes and ladders'.

1206 Qutb-ud-Din Aybak established the Delhi Sultanate in India. He was a slave who rose to the postion of military commander in the army of Muhammad of Ghur. Qutb-ud-Din set up headquarters in Lahore (present-day Pakistan) and Delhi. He laid the foundation of the famous stone tower Qutb Minar in Delhi.

1210 The Franciscan order was founded by Francis of Assisi with the approval of Pope Innocent III.

***c.*1214** North German towns and German trading communities formed an association called the Hanseatic League. The League controlled most of the trading activities in northern Europe for the following two centuries.

1215 King John was forced by English barons to sign the Magna Carta, a document that limited the king's power and gave the people certain basic rights.

▶ *Genghis Khan unified the nomadic tribes of Mongolia and founded a vast Mongolian Empire. The great warrior-ruler extended his empire across Asia to the Adriatic Sea.*

1220-1250

1220 Frederick II became Holy Roman emperor. He angered Pope Honorius III because of his delay in departing for the Fifth Crusade.

1220–1223 Genghis Khan attacked and destroyed the city of Samarkand in Central Asia. He then sent two of his best generals to defeat an army of Russians and Kipchak Turks.

***c.*1220–1292** British scientist and philosopher Roger Bacon lived during this period. He was the first European to describe the process of making gunpowder and proposed motorized ships and flying machines.

▼ *The procedure for the papal Inquisition allowed a person accused of heresy time to confess and clear himself.*

1228–1229 Frederick II set off on the Sixth Crusade. He obtained Bethlehem, Nazareth and Jerusalem from the Egyptian sultan through diplomatic negotiations and military threats.

1231 Pope Gregory IX initiated the Catholic Inquisition to discover and punish heretics (those who opposed official Church doctrine).

*c.***1237** Mongol warriors led by Sabutai, a son of Genghis Khan, conquered attacked Russia, then Poland.

1238 Muhammad I established the Nasrid dynasty in Granada, Spain. The dynasty ruled the area for 260 years and played an important part in the Islamic struggle against Christianity in Spain.

▲ *Holy Roman emperor Frederick II led a successful Crusade.*

1241 Following a dispute with Pope Gregory IX, the Holy Roman emperor Frederick II invaded the Papal States and captured a number of clergymen. Frederick II later tried to make peace with Pope Innocent IV, but his attempt failed. His struggle with the papacy continued and the new Pope Innocent IV declared that the emperor was excommunicated and deposed. Only a few nobles accepted that the pope had the right to depose the emperor, so the dispute dragged on until Frederick's death in 1250. The German nobles then began a civil war to see who would become the new Emperor.

*c.***1250** The Toltec-Chichimec people took control of Cholula, in Mexico, and built new ceremonial structures around the Pyramid of Quetzalcóatl.

1254-1328

1254–1324 Venetian merchant and traveller Marco Polo lived during this period. He travelled to China and spent years in the court of Kublai Khan.

1258 The Mongol army led by Hülegü Khan destroyed Baghdad, killed several of its inhabitants and brought an end to the Abbasid Caliphate here.

1272 Edward I ascended the English throne. He instituted administrative and legal reforms, and conquered north Wales.

1290 Osman I became leader of the Seljuk Turks. He established the Islamic town of Bithynia, from which grew the great Ottoman Empire.

1292 Edward I, King of England, defeated the Scottish army at Dunbar, imprisoned Scots King John de Balliol and took control of Scotland.

1297 Scottish patriot William Wallace defeated the English forces in the Battle of Stirling. He was later defeated in the Battle of Falkirk and executed.

***c.*1300** Various tribes migrated from the northern parts of the American southwest towards the Little Colorado River and the Rio Grande in the south to establish the Kachina cult.

1314 Scottish forces led by Robert Bruce defeated English king Edward II in the Battle of Bannockburn.

> ### ...FASCINATING FACT...
> For years before his great victory at Bannockburn in 1314, Robert Bruce was a fugitive from the English. On one occasion he had decided to give up while hiding in a cave, but was inspired to continue by the perseverance of a spider building a web.

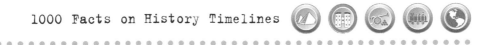
*c.***1325** The Aztecs settled on a marshy island in Lake Texcoco, Mexico, and founded the city of Tenochtitlán.

1328 Philip VI ascended the French throne and established the Valois dynasty. He continued efforts to centralize the state, but made concessions to the nobility and clergy.

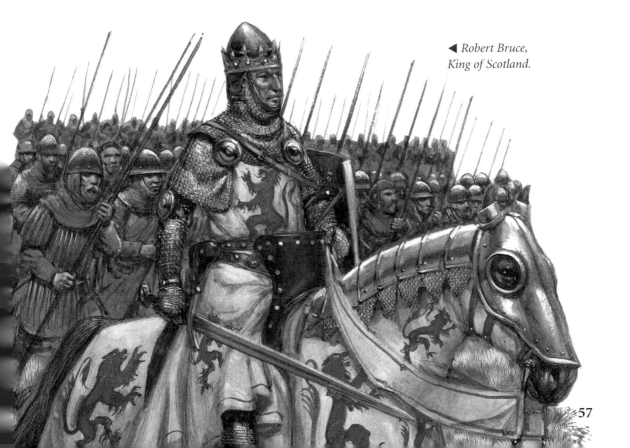

◀ *Robert Bruce, King of Scotland.*

57

1333–1348

◀ *Plague is transmitted by the bite of the rat flea.*

***c.*1333** Drought, famine and the Black Death, a fatal disease, struck China.

***c.*1333** Arabian traveller and explorer Ibn Battutah came to India. He spent 27 years travelling through Asia, Africa and Europe, covering a distance of 120,000 km. He wrote one of the most famous travel books, the *Rihlah*.

1333 In Japan, the Kamakura shoguns were removed from power and Emperor Go-Daigo. Emperor Komyo, later appointed Ashikaga Takauji as shogun, thus restoring the power of the shoguns. The rule of the Ashikaga is known as the Muromachi period.

1335 The first public mechanical clock was erected in Milan, Italy.

1336–1614 The Vijayanagara Empire in south India extended over parts of present-day Andhra Pradesh and Karnataka. They had a rich architectural and sculptural tradition, traces of which can be seen in the ruined city of Hampi in Karnataka.

1337 The Hundred Years War started between England and France when Edward III invaded Flanders to stake his claim over the French crown.

1340 Alfonso XI of Castile crushed an army of Spanish and Moroccan muslims with the help of the Portuguese.

1346 An English army of 12,000 troops commanded by Edward III defeated 30,000 French troops in the Battle of Crécy because of superior weaponry and tactics.

1346 Scotland's David II, an ally of Philip VI, invaded England, but was captured and imprisoned.

1348 The Black Death, which had already spread in Cyprus, reached Florence. It then spread across Europe.

▶ *The Black Death plague originated in Central Asia and from there spread to Constantinople and Mediterranean ports. By the 14th century, the plague had reached Europe.*

1349–1360

1349 The Black Death spread to England. Nearly half of England's population was wiped out because of the disease, causing widespread social and economic problems. England was not in a position to continue its conflict with France and had to call a truce.

1349 The Black Death spread to Poland and Russia.

1350 The Pueblo Indians of the southwest of North America formed a few large settlements.

1350 Alfonso X of Castile died of the plague.

1350 Philip VI, King of France, died and was succeeded by his son John II.

1352 The Black Death spread back to India and China after claiming the lives of hundreds of Russians.

1354 After recovering from the Black Death, England continued the Hundred Years War by raiding Languedoc in southern France.

1356 France was defeated in the Battle of Poitiers by the Black Prince of Wales. King John II of France and several of his courtiers were captured and imprisoned in England. Charles, John's eldest son, was made regent of France, but was unable to prevent the civil war that followed, and eventually fled Paris.

1358 France was torn apart with a violent revolt by thousands of peasants.

...FASCINATING FACT...
In 1392 the French painter Jacques Gringonneur was commissioned to paint playing cards for the king of France. The pack of 52 cards contained four suits. The spades stood for soldiers, diamonds for craftsmen, clubs for farmers and hearts for the clergy.

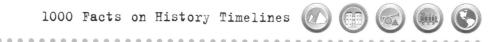

◀ *Higher taxes were imposed by the state on the peasants of France. This, coupled with an increase of rents by landlords, led to a revolt in the country.*

1360 The English and the French signed a treaty, the Peace of Bretigny. Charles agreed to give England Calais, Guienne and Ponthieu as well as three million gold crowns as ransom money. King John of France was released but returned voluntarily to England when the money could not be raised.

1368-1405

▶ *Edward the Black Prince never ruled as king because of his early death at the age of 45.*

1368 The Ming dynasty came to power in China, providing a boost to arts such as landscape and figure painting, ceramics and metalwork.

1369 British poet Geoffrey Chaucer produced his first major work, *Book of the Duchess*.

1377 Richard II ascended the English throne. Born in 1367, he was the son of Edward the Black Prince and Joan, the Fair Maid of Kent. Richard was only ten years old when he succeeded his grandfather, Edward III.

1381 In England, farm labourers and artisans revolted against the poll tax and low wages. Richard II agreed to abolish some taxes and reduce others, but later went back on his word.

1385 John I founded the Aviz dynasty in Portugal after defeating Castile in the Battle of Aljubarrota.

1389 The Ottoman Turks, led by Murad I, defeated the Serbians in the Battle of Kosovo. This victory secured Ottoman control of the Balkans.

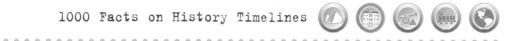

▲ *Chaucer's* Canterbury Tales *is a collection of tales told by a group of fictional pilgrims on their way from Southwark to Canterbury in England.*

1391 Aztec ruler Huitzilihuitl made the Aztecs independent in Mexico.

1398 Mongol king Timur (or Tamerlane) invaded India. He sacked Delhi and ended the Tughluq dynasty.

***c.*1400** Sri Lanka was divided into the Kotte, Kandy and Jaffna regions. The first two were Sinhalese kingdoms and the last was a Tamil kingdom.

***c.*1405–1407** Chinese admiral and diplomat Zheng He visited southern Vietnam, Thailand, Malacca, Java and Sri Lanka.

63

1410–1429

1410 The K'iche' Mayans of Central America expanded their kingdom to include a large part of the Guatemala.

1413 Muhammad I, son of Bayazid I, became the ruler of the Ottoman Empire after a civil war following his father's death.

1415 An English army led by Henry V defeated the French in the Battle of Agincourt. Henry V then forced the French to sign the Treaty of Troyes, which named him heir to the French throne.

1416 The fleet of the Ottoman Turks was defeated by Venice at Dardanelles.

1420 Sesshu, the Japanese master of ink painting, *suiboku*, was born. Adapting the Chinese style of landscape painting, he set the standard in ink painting.

1421 Murad II extended the Ottoman empire into southeastern Europe. He defeated the Byzantine king Manuel II Palaeologus and forced him to pay tribute to the Ottoman Empire.

***c.*1422** The Chinese fleet led by Admiral Zheng made expeditions to new countries around the Indian Ocean.

1422 Henry VI became king of England. As son of Henry V and Catherine Valois he was proclaimed king of France, in accordance with the terms of the Treaty of Troyes. However, many Frenchmen refused to accept Henry and declared Charles' son to be King Charles VII.

***c.*1427** In Mexico, Tenochtitlán, Tlacopan and Texcoco formed the Triple Alliance, which defeated Azcapotzalco and established the Aztec Empire. Tenochtitlán became the leading city of Mexico.

1429 Joan of Arc freed Orléans from the English. Teenage Joan claimed to hear the voice of the Archangel Michael telling her to free France and return Charles VII to the throne.

▼ *The French army suffered a disastrous defeat at the hands of the English in the Battle of Agincourt in 1415, in spite of having more men and superior armour.*

1431-1460

1431 Angkor, the capital of the Khmer Empire of Cambodia, was destroyed by people from Thailand. The Khmer Empire ended .

1438 In Peru, Emperor Pachacuti established the Inca Empire.

*c.***1441** Portuguese traders and colonists first brought African slaves to Lisbon, where they were sold in the markets.

1443 Poland, Hungary and Serbia came together to fight the Ottoman Turks. They had some victories, but Ottoman sultan Murad II defeated them in the Battle of Zlatica, in the Balkans.

*c.***1446** Korean king Sejong proclaimed the Korean Hangul alphabet as the official script, replacing the Chinese script that had been in use until then.

1450 The French defeated the English army at the Battle of Formigny and reoccupied Normandy.

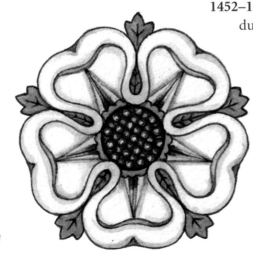

1452–1519 Leonardo da Vinci lived during this period. He was a talented Renaissance painter, sculptor and inventor, who was born in the town of Vinci near Florence. *Mona Lisa* and *The Last Supper* are two of his most famous paintings.

◀ *The white rose, the symbol of the House of York.*

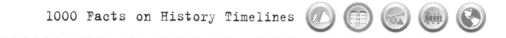

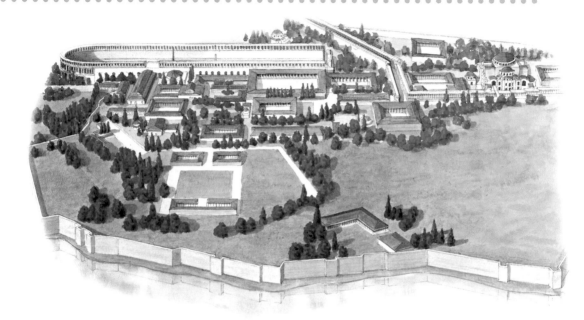

▲ *Constantinople was renamed Istanbul after it was captured by the Ottoman Empire.*

1453 Ottoman Turks led by Muhammad II defeated Constantine XI Palaeologus, the last Byzantine emperor, and captured Constantinople. This marked the end of the Byzantine Empire.

1455 In England, the Duke of York led his forces against those of King Henry VI. York won the Battle at St Albans, thus starting the civil wars that became known as the Wars of the Roses.

1455 Johannes Gutenberg of Germany published the first book printed using fully moveable type – the Bible.

1461–1492

1461 Edward, the new duke of York, defeated the Lancastrians at Mortimer's Cross, and later at Towton. The English Parliament declared him king of England and he ruled as Edward IV.

1467–1477 In Japan, the Onin War broke out between two rival clans, leading to a century of turmoil and violence, as feudal lords rose to power.

1471–1528 German painter and printmaker Albrecht Dürer lived during this period. He was well-known for his paintings and for prints made from woodcuts.

1475–1564 Italian artist Michelangelo lived during this period. He was a painter, sculptor, poet and architect. Some of his most famous works are the statue of *David* and the Sistine chapel paintings.

1478 The growing power of the Tarascan and Aztec Empires in Central America resulted in wars in which the Aztecs were the victors.

1480 Louis XI of France brought Anjou, Bar, Maine and Provence under direct royal control.

1483–1520 Italian painter and architect Raphael lived during this period. His most famous works include his paintings of Madonna and his large figure compositions in the papal apartments at the Vatican in Rome.

1485 Lancastrian Henry Tudor, Earl of Richmond, fought and defeated Richard III, brother of Edward IV, in the Battle of Bosworth.

*c.***1490** In India, Guru Nanak Dev established the Sikh religion.

1492 Italian-Spanish explorer Christopher Columbus landed in the Bahamas and so became the first European to cross the Atlantic.

◄ *This marble sculpture called* David *was made by Italian artist Michelangelo.*

1497–1506

◄ *The voyages of Portuguese navigator Vasco da Gama to India laid open the sea route to the East from Europe and helped Portugal establish a flourishing trade.*

1497–1498 Spanish explorer Amerigo Vespucci navigated an exploration of the North American landmass. He also led a second expedition to Guyana and the mouth of the Amazon. The Americas were been named after him.

1498 The Portuguese explorer Vasco da Gama arrived in India. His route took him round the Cape of Good Hope, past the easternmost point reached by explorer Bartolomew Dias in 1488. This voyage opened up a way for Europeans to reach the wealth of the Indies, and out of it grew the Portuguese Empire.

1498 Spanish colonists arrived in the Caribbean island Hispaniola, which was later divided into Haiti and the Dominican Republic. After killing the natives, the Spanish settled there bringing with them African slaves to carry out hard labour for them.

1502 The Islamic Safavid dynasty of Persia came to power in Azerbaijan.

1502 Montezuma II became the Aztec emperor. His reign was marked by warfare, and he made enemies of neighbouring tribes and peoples. When Cortés arrived in Mexico he was able to gain allies among Montezuma's enemies. Montezuma thought the Spanish were descendants of a god and tried to coax them into leaving with rich gifts. Montezuma's name is linked to fabulous treasures that the Spanish stole from the Aztecs.

1505 The first Portuguese trading post in Sri Lanka was established at Colombo.

1505 In Poland, the national diet (parliament) took charge of running the country. The members of the diet were elected by Polish nobility.

1505 Francisco de Almeida of Portugal conquered the African kingdoms of Quiloa and Mombasa. He then went on to India and established forts at Calicut, Cannanore and Cochin on the east coast.

1506 Donato Bramante, the great Renaissance architect and painter, began the construction of Saint Peter's Basilica at Rome.

1507 Zafi in Morocco was captured by the Portuguese, who began to export Moorish, Berber and Jewish slaves from there.

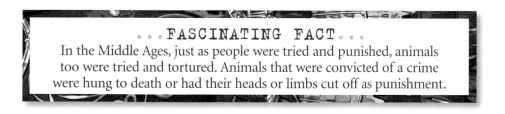

. . . FASCINATING FACT . . .
In the Middle Ages, just as people were tried and punished, animals too were tried and tortured. Animals that were convicted of a crime were hung to death or had their heads or limbs cut off as punishment.

1509-1513

1509 Henry VII of England died and his son Henry VIII ascended the English throne. Henry VIII was educated in the teachings of the Renaissance.

1509–1510 Spaniards explored the South American landmass, reaching. Colombia and Darién.

1510 Ismail Safavi of Persia extended his empire to the River Oxus by defeating the Uzbeks and capturing Herat, Bactria and Khiva.

1510 The Portuguese conquered Goa on the Malabar Coast and took control of the spice trade in India.

1511 The Strait of Malacca and the port of Malacca were under the control of the Portuguese, who offered the Thai kingdom of Ayudhya firearms in return for trading rights.

1511 African slaves were sent to Cuba to work as labourers.

1512 The Ottoman sultan Bayazid II died and his son Selim I came to power.

1513 Italian Niccolo Machiavelli wrote *The Prince*, a book on how to govern.

> ## ...FASCINATING FACT...
> Frescoes are paintings done on plaster. There are two types of frescoes – buon fresco and secco fresco. In the buon fresco the surface has to be prepared with at least three layers of plaster, the last one usually made of marble dust. The painting is done with water-based pigments that are applied before the plaster dries, so that the colours dry along with plaster, making them last longer. A secco fresco is painted on dry plaster. In this technique colours are not very bright or long-lasting.

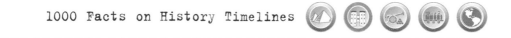

▲ *Henry VIII and Anne Boleyn (left) at the royal court.*

1513 James IV of Scotland was defeated and killed by the English in the Battle of Flodden.

1513 The Portuguese were the first Europeans to reach China via the sea route.

1514 Ottoman sultan Selim I defeated the Safavid shah Ismail and captured the Persian capital Tabriz. He forced the Shia Muslims of Persia to accept the Sunni faith.

1515 France defeated the Swiss and Venetian forces of the Holy League in the Battle of Marignano.

1516–1517 Selim I, the Ottoman sultan, conquered Syria and Egypt. With Mecca under their control, the Ottomans undertook the construction of mosques, hospitals and public buildings in the area and organized annual pilgrimages to the holy shrine located there. This gave the Ottoman rulers immense prestige in the Muslim world.

▼ *In 1519 the Spanish conquistador Hernando Cortés led a group of 600 men into Mexico. They were able to conquer the Aztec Empire in less than two years.*

1517 Martin Luther, a German monk, began the Reformation movement in Wittenberg, Germany. He protested against the Roman Church's misuse of power. It was the beginning of a long period of religious conflict in Europe and led to the formation of Protestant churches. Luther was educated at the cathedral school at Eisenach and later at the University of Erfurt. In 1505 he completed his master's examination and began the study of law. He gave up his career in law and said his true calling was in religion.

1519–1521 Spanish conquistador Hernando Cortés arrived in Mexico. He attacked the Aztec's capital Tenochtitlán. Aztec king Montezuma II was captured during the attack.

1519–1521 Portuguese-born Spanish explorer Ferdinand Magellan set out to explore Asia. He arrived at the Philippine Islands after sailing across the Pacific Ocean. Magellan was killed by the Mactan people who lived in the Philippines. His ship later returned to Spain.

1520 Ottoman sultan Selim I died. He was succeeded by his son Suleiman I, also known as Suleiman the Magnificent. Suleiman captured Belgrade and made it his base to raid deep into Hungary.

1522 Cuauhtémoc, the last Aztec ruler, was captured and killed by the Spaniards with the help of the Tlaxcalans, enemies of the Aztecs. The city of Tenochtitlán was destroyed and the Aztec Empire came to an end.

1522 The Portuguese were expelled from China.

1522 Martin Luther and Huldrych Zwingli published new books to promote the Reformation movement.

1523 Sweden freed itself from Denmark. Gustav I, who established the house of Vasa, was crowned king of Sweden.

1523-1526

1523 Huayna Capac, ruler of the Peruvian Inca Empire, passed away. His kingdom was divided between his two sons, Atahualpa and Huáscar.

1524 Reformation preacher Thomas Münzer asked the peasants in Germany to rebel against their feudal rulers and all Catholics, resulting in violent fighting and great loss of life.

1524 Spanish conquistador Francisco Pizarro set out to search for a rumoured civilization in South America, the Incas.

1525 Spanish and German forces defeated France in the Battle of Pavia. Francis I of France, was taken prisoner.

1525 Albert von Brandenburg, the Grand Master of the Teutonic Knights, became a Protestant and declared himself owner of the lands of the Teutonic Knights with the title, Duke of Prussia. He thus established Prussia as a country.

1525 Southern Athapaskan peoples of Canada migrated to the Southwest of North America. They later split into groups such as the Apache and Navajo.

1526 In India, Babar, the ruler of Kabul, defeated Ibrahim Lodi, the sultan ruling over Delhi, in the first Battle of Panipat. Babar established the Mughal dynasty in India.

1526 Ottoman sultan Suleiman killed Louis II of Hungary in the Battle of Mohács and took all his lands. The Ottoman Empire reached the height of its power during the reign of Suleiman.

1526 Ferdinand, younger brother of Emperor Charles V, was crowned king of Bohemia. He faced rival claimants in Hungary and periodically fought against the Ottoman Empire.

1527 Pope Clement VII allied with France. The Holy Roman emperor Charles V captured Rome and had Clement VII imprisoned for months.

▶ *The Inca mountain city of Machu Picchu was a forgotten marvel, lost for 400 years.*

1528-1533

1528 Jacob Hutter, an Austrian preacher, established the Protestant sect of Hutterites. The Hutterites moved to Hungary and Ukraine.

1529 Mughal emperor Babar defeated the Afghan chieftains ruling over the eastern Indian states of Bihar and Bengal. His empire stretched from Kabul in the west to Bengal in the east.

1529 Martin Luther's protest against the Catholic Church's ban on his teachings led to the Reformation movement being named Protestantism.

1529 The Ottoman Turks conquered Algeria and invaded Hungary. King John Zapolya now ruled Hungary as an Ottoman puppet.

1530 The Knights Hospitaller of Saint John settled on the island of Malta, which was given to them by Charles V. They became known as the Knights of Malta.

1531 Protestant princes and imperial cities of Europe came together to form the Schmalkaldic League against the Holy Roman emperor Charles V. The objective of the league was to protect the newly formed Lutheran churches from being attacked by Charles V and other Catholics.

> ### ...FASCINATING FACT...
> In medieval Europe, babies were wrapped tightly in cloth until they were six months old. It was considered unhealthy for them to move their hands and legs! Until the age of six, boys and girls were both dressed in frocks. Once a boy was six years old, he was given his first pair of breeches. 'Breeching' was an important occasion and called for celebration. A feast was arranged and family and friends got together to celebrate.

1533 England's Henry VIII married Anne Boleyn. The marriage followed Henry's divorce from his first wife, Katherine of Aragon. The divorce was not approved by the pope, so England became Protestant.

1533 Ivan IV (also known as Ivan the Terrrible) became the grand duke of Moscow and assumed the title of Tsar, meaning 'emperor'. He carried out a series of reforms and centralized the administration.

1533 Spanish adventurer Francisco Pizarro invaded Peru and had Inca ruler Atahualpa killed. The Inca began a war that would last for generations.

▶ *During the reign of Suleiman I, the Ottoman Empire reached its peak. It included most of the major Muslim cities and extended to the Balkans and Hungary.*

79

1534–1542

▲ *1539 saw the dissolution (closing down) of Roman Catholic monastries in England and Wales. The property was sold off to nobles, raising money for Henry VIII.*

1534 Ottoman sultan Suleiman I took over the Persian city of Tabriz and extended his kingdom to include Iraq.

1534 Ignatius Loyola founded the counter-Reformation Roman Catholic order of the Society of Jesus, or the Jesuits, in Paris.

1535 The Sforza dynasty in Milan ended with the death of Francesco Sforza II. Milan came under the control of the Holy Roman emperor Charles V.

1536–1598 Japanese shogun Toyotomi Hideyoshi lived during this period. He totally reformed Japanese government.

1538 The Ottoman Turks led by the admiral Khayr ad-din defeated the combined forces of Venice, the Holy Roman emperor Charles V and Pope Paul III in a naval battle, and took control of the Mediterranean. Khayr ad-din dominated the Mediterranean for 20 years.

1540 In India, Afghan king Sher Shah Suri defeated the Mughal emperor Humayun and drove him out of India. Sher Shah died in 1545. Humayun returned to Delhi and re-established the Mughal Empire.

1541 Scots lawyer John Knox took the Reformation movement to Scotland. He was also the founder of the Presbyterian Church.

1541 After discovering the Gulf of Lawrence and founding a French colony in Canada, the French explorer Jacques Cartier explored much of North America and established a French colony at Quebec.

1541–1614 Spanish painter El Greco lived during this period. He was the first great master of Spanish painting.

1542 Henry VIII defeated James V of Scotland in the Battle of Solway Moss. The Scottish king died soon thereafter and was succeeded by his infant daughter, Mary Queen of Scots.

1543-1555

◄ *Edward VI, King of England and Ireland, had an uneventful reign and eventually died as a minor, apparently due to tuberculosis.*

1543 Portuguese sailors arrived on the island of Tanegashima in Japan. They established trade through the port of Nagasaki, supplying firearms and tobacco among other things.

1543 Polish astronomer Nicolaus Copernicus published theories that stated that the Earth and other planets rotated on their own axes and revolved in orbits around the Sun. This is generally termed as the heliocentric (or 'Sun-centred') system.

1547 The English forces defeated the Scottish army in the Battle of Pinkie. The English army occupied Scottish towns and castles for several years, until a peace was agreed.

1549 Christianity gained popularity in Japan due to the efforts of the Jesuit priest Francis Xavier.

1550 In North America, the Mohawk, Oneida, Onondaga, Cayuga and Seneca tribes came together to form the League of the Iroquois.

1551 France began its war against Holy Roman emperor Charles V yet again by capturing Toul, Metz and Verdun in the Lorraine region.

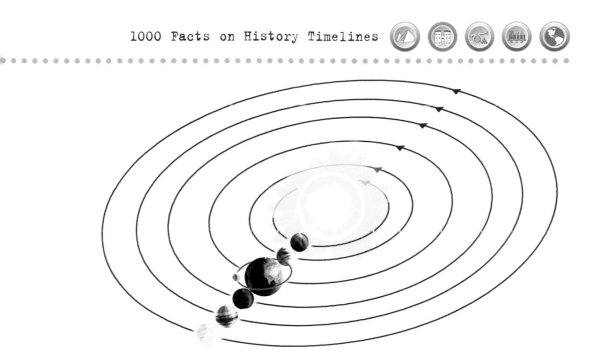

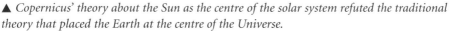

▲ *Copernicus' theory about the Sun as the centre of the solar system refuted the traditional theory that placed the Earth at the centre of the Universe.*

1552 Ivan IV, the Tsar of Moscow, expanded his kingdom by capturing the Tatar city of Kazan. He then proceeded to invade Astrakhan, a city in southern Russia.

1553 Edward VI, King of England, passed away. Mary Tudor succeeded him. She married King Philip II of Spain, son of Charles V, and re-established the Roman Catholic church in England.

1555 German Catholics and Protestants ended their fight with the Religious Peace of Augsburg, according to which each state had the freedom to decide on the religion it would follow.

1556-1568

▶ *The English secret service uncovered the role of Mary, Queen of Scots in a Catholic plot and she was beheaded at Fotheringay Castle in February 1587.*

1556 Mughal emperor Akbar came to the throne. He reorganized the administration of his empire, encouraged arts and literature and conquered Bengal, Kashmir and Deccan.

1557 The Portuguese began trading with the Chinese mainland.

1557 Spanish forces drove the French out of Italy after defeating them in the Battle of St Quentin.

1558 Elizabeth I ascended the English throne. Her reign saw art and literature flourish, but her Protestant faith caused friction with Catholic states.

1562 Civil war broke out in France following the mass murder of Huguenots (Protestants) by Catholics.

1564 Maximilian II became the Holy Roman emperor. He worked for the reform of the Roman Catholic Church.

1564–1616 English poet and playwright William Shakespeare lived during this period. *Macbeth, Othello, Romeo and Juliet* and *A Midsummer Night's Dream* are some of his plays.

1565 In India, the Bahmani sultans, ruling princely states in the Deccan, raided and destroyed the south Indian Vijayanagar kingdom.

1567 Scottish noblemen forced Mary Queen of Scots to step down from the Scottish throne.

1568 In Japan, Oda Nobunaga ended the rule of the Ashikaga shogunate.

1569–1584

1569 In France, Catholic forces defeated Huguenot forces in the Battle of Jarnac. The Catholic troops under Marshal Gaspard de Tavannes surprised and defeated the Huguenots, who were being led by Gaspard de Coligny and the prince of Condé. The prince of Condé was executed after the battle. Coligny escaped by reorganizing his troops and retreating to the south. He was defeated at Moncontour the same year.

1570 Ivan the Terrible, tsar of Moscow, captured the great city of Novgorod in northwestern Russia. He destroyed many of the buildings in the city and killed thousands of its citizens.

1571 The combined naval forces of Spain, Venice, Genoa and Malta defeated the Ottoman fleet in the Battle of Lepanto. The battle was fought near the Gulf of Patras off the port of Lepanto, Greece. The combined fleet had 250 galleys carrying about 30,000 men. Nearly 15,000 Turks were killed or taken prisoners along with 200 ships. The victors lost over 7000 men.

▶ Lepanto was the last great battle between fleets of galleys – warships powered by huge banks of oarsmen.

1571 German astronomer Johannes Kepler was born in this year. He won a scholarship to the University of Tübingen where he studied to be a Lutheran priest. It was here that he was first introduced to the ideas of the astronomer Copernicus, which put the Sun, not the Earth, at the centre of the solar system. Kepler is famous for his laws of planetary motion. He was also the first to investigate the formation of pictures with a pin hole camera, and to formulate different eyeglass designs for short-sightedness and long-sightedness.

1572 Thousands of Huguenots were killed by the Catholics of France on the orders of King Charles IX, in the Massacre of St Bartholomew. The religious wars began again in France.

1576 In Spanish-ruled Netherlands, 17 Protestant provinces came together to form the Pacification of Ghent, in their war against the Spanish Inquisition.

1577 Flemish painter Peter Paul Ruebens was born. He was well educated as he came from a wealthy lawyer's family. After school, he served as a page in the royal court at Antwerp. Ruebens went on to become the leading artist of his time and influenced many artists.

1578 Mongolian ruler Altan Khan gave the leader of the Gelukpa Buddhist monastery in Drepung, Tibet, the title of Dalai Lama. The Dalai Lama is the spiritual leader of Tibet and is much respected by Tibetans even today.

1582 Pope Gregory XIII introduced the new, more accurate, Gregorian calendar, replacing the older Julian calendar. It was several decades before all European countries adopted the new system.

1584 English navigator Sir Walter Raleigh founded the Virginia colony on Roanoke Island in North America. Raleigh is also remembered in anecdotes as having once laid his cloak on a muddy puddle so that Queen Elizabeth wouldn't get her shoes dirty.

1586–1595

1586 Hideyoshi was made the Shogun of Japan by the emperor Goyozei. The following year Hideyoshi defeated the Japanese feudal rulers (*daimyo*s) and brought them under his control.

1587 Mary Queen of Scots was executed by Elizabeth I of England after she plotted to kill Elizabeth and seize her throne. Mary became queen of Scotland after her father's death, when she was only six days old. Although she was renowned for her beauty and kind heart, she lacked the political skills to rule Scotland with success. She was forced to abdicate in favour of her infant son James I. Mary then fled to England hoping that her cousin Elizabeth I would help her. But Elizabeth was afraid that Mary would take over the English throne with help from the Catholics. Mary was imprisoned, and Elizabeth ordered that all Mary's possessions be burned. Eventually, Mary was beheaded for treason. Upon Elizabeth's death in 1603, Mary's son became king of England.

1587 In Persia, the Safavid ruler Abbas I came to power. He is considered the greatest of the Safavid rulers. During his reign, art and architecture flowered administration of the country was reorganized and foreign trade was encouraged.

1588 The English defeated the Spanish Armada. King Philip II of Spain had sent the 130-ship Armada to conquer Protestant England and make himself king of England.

1589 Huguenot leader Henry of Navarre ascended the throne of France as Henry IV. He defeated the Catholic League in the Battle of Ivry, fought in Normandy. Henry's forces went on to lay siege to Paris, where they were defeated. Despite this setback, Henry IV became the legitimate successor to the throne after the death of his cousin, Henry III of France. The new king was unpopular in the south, and not trusted by many in the army. The rest of the

country refused to recognize him as king as he had been excommunicated by the Pope. Later Henry became a Catholic and so was accepted as king.

1595 The Ottoman sultan Murad III died. His eldest son Mohammed III succeeded him. His weak rule marked the beginning of the downfall of the Ottoman Empire.

▶ *The ill-fated Spanish Armada suffered a decisive defeat at the hands of the English army and had to also battle storms on the way back to Spain.*

1597–1607

1597 The first-ever opera was written. The word 'opera' is a Latin word meaning 'works'. It is the plural of *opus* since it combined solo and choral singing, drama and dancing in a staged spectacle. The earliest work considered an opera is *Dafne*, written by Jacopo Peri.

1598 Fyodor I, the Tsar of Moscow, died. The last of the Riurikovich dynasty, Fyodor was born mentally challenged and was a mere figurehead. Russia had already been devastated by the excesses of his father, Ivan the Terrible.

1598 Henry IV and Philip II ended the war between France and Spain by signing the Treaty of Vervins.

1598 Spain's Philip II passed away. He was succeeded by his son Philip III, during whose reign the Spanish economy suffered. Agricultural production declined and unemployment and poverty increased.

1600 The British East India Company was formed. The company was popularly known as John Company, and was founded by a Royal Charter of Elizabeth I. Over the next 250 years, the East India Company became one of the most powerful commercial enterprises of its time.

...FASCINATING FACT...
In medieval Japan, warriors called samurai began the practice of ritual suicide or hara-kiri (*seppuko*). A samurai committed hara-kiri by cutting open his stomach. Hara-kiri was committed for a number of reasons, including proving one's loyalty to one's master, expressing sorrow, as a method of punishing oneself, or to prevent oneself from being captured.

1600 Tokugawa Ieyasu became ruler of Japan after defeating other rivals for the throne in the Battle of Sekigahara. The Tokugawas ruled Japan till 1867, a period during which the country was peaceful and prosperous.

1605 A group of Roman Catholic rebels plotted to blow up the Houses of Parliament in London. The 'Gunpowder Plot' was discovered and Guy Fawkes, one of the main conspirators, was executed. After the plot, the Protestant government ordered a crackdown on Catholics.

1606 Australia had her first European visitors when a Dutch expedition arrived at the Cape York Peninsula. They were driven away by the natives.

1606 Rembrandt van Rijn, the famous Dutch painter who specialized in portraits and biblical scenes, was born.

1607 The first successful British colony in North America was established in the Chesapeake Bay area. It was named Jamestown after the king of England, James I. In 1608, the fort at Jamestown, Virginia, was destroyed by fire and several colonists died of starvation and disease.

▲ *The Japanese warrior caste Samurai held bravery, honour and loyalty to one's master even above life.*

1608–1612

◀ *After his unsuccessful uprising against the English forces, Hugh O'Neill, earl of Tyrone, spent the rest of his life in Rome.*

1608 Matthias took over the leadership of the Hapsburg House from his mentally unstable brother Rudolf II, the Holy Roman emperor.

1608 Samuel de Champlain founded a French settlement at Quebec, Canada.

1609 Philip III of Spain expelled 275,000 Moriscos (Moors converted to Christianity) for practicing Islam secretly. The Moors had contributed greatly to the development of Spanish art, architecture, literature and culture. The Spanish economy suffered a serious short-term decline.

1609 Johannes Kepler discovered that planets move around the Sun on elliptical paths and at different speeds. Kepler had initially believed that celestial objects moved in perfect circles.

1611 English forces drove Hugh O'Neill, the rebellious earl of Tyrone, out of Ireland and annexed Ulster to the British kingdom.

1611 Charles IX of Sweden passed away and was succeeded by his son Gustavus II Adolphus. The new king increased the powers of the Swedish Council and gave it a more important role in running the country.

1612 Mughal emperor Jahangir gave the English East India Company permission to trade in India after two of their ships defeated four Portuguese galleons at Surat.

1612 England established Londonderry in Northern Ireland. Land was given away to Protestants who were supporters of the English throne.

▼ *The Alcazar Fortress was originally built by the Moors, who introduced Islamic architecture in Spain.*

93

1613–1624

▼ *Cervantes'* Don Quixote *relates the tale of an elderly knight who sets out to seek adventure in the company of his squire and his horse.*

1613 Russian noblemen, or boyars, elected Mikhail Romanov (the first of the Romanov rulers) as the Tsar of Russia. His election ended eight years of political chaos in Russia.

1615 Part II of Cervantes' *Don Quixote* was published. The author was 58 years old. *Don Quixote* was an enormous and immediate success and became a classic of Spanish literature.

1616 Manchurian forces led by Nurhachi invaded China. Nurhachi laid the foundations of the Ch'ing dynasty that later replaced the Chinese Mings.

1617 Philip III sent Don García de Silva y Figueroa as Spanish ambassador to the Safavid court at Isfahan, Persia, establishing diplomatic links between Christian and Muslim countries for the first time.

1618 Roman Catholic governors of Bohemia shut down Protestant chapels. Angry Protestants threw two governors from a window in Hradcany Palacc. This incident, which is referred to as the 'Defenestration of Prague', led to the Thirty Years War between France, Sweden, Spain and the Holy Roman Empire, among other countries.

1619 African slaves were brought to Virginia to work on tobacco, rice and indigo plantations.

1620 The ship *Mayflower* sailed to America. On board were radical English Protestants, known as Puritans. They founded Plymouth colony, where they could practice their religion freely.

1622 Native Americans attacked several settlements in Virginia and killed more than 300 colonists.

1622 Persian Safavid ruler Abbas controlled trade in the Persian Gulf with the help of the British East India Company. They drove out the Portuguese, who had previously controlled the area.

1624 Dutch settlers bought Manhattan from local tribes and renamed it New Amsterdam. According to legend, the island was bought from the natives in exchange for beads and other trinkets.

▶ *The Native American Hopi people of Arizonaare, descendants of the Pueblo Indian group.*

1625–1629

1625 The Huguenots of France rose in revolt against the Catholic government. Charles I of England sent ships to France to help Louis XIII fight against the Huguenots.

1626 French colonizers settled in Madagascar and began to drive out the Hovas who had been on the island for 600 years.

1626 The Thirty Years War continued with Catholic forces winning the Battle of Dessau. The defeated Danish forces fled to Hungary. The Catholic forces then conquered Holstein, Schleswig, Jutland, Mecklenburg and Pomerania in northeastern Germany.

▶ *Oliver Cromwell became Lord Protector. Here, Bible in hand, he makes a rousing speech to his Roundhead troops. Both sides in the English Civil War believed that they were fighting for God.*

1627 Korea was invaded by the Manchurians of China and brought under their control. The invaders withdrew only after they were granted certain concessions.

1627 In central India, Shivaji Bhonsle founded the Maratha kingdom, which was very powerful in north and south India during the 17th century.

1628 Huguenot power in France ended when they surrendered at La Rochelle, after the town had been surrounded and continuously attacked by French Catholic forces for 14 months.

1629 Abbas, the shah of Persia, died and was succeeded by his grandson Safi I. He had most of his relatives killed, so there could be no other claimant to the throne. Meanwhile, the Uzbeks captured Kandahar, the first capital of Afghanistan.

1629 The English Parliament was dissolved by Charles I, who for the following 11 years ruled without calling a Parliament.

1629 The Holy Roman emperor Ferdinand II and Christian IV of Denmark called a truce and signed the Treaty of Lübeck. According to the treaty, Denmark got back the duchy of Holstein and promised to keep out of Germany.

1630 New settlers arrived in North America and founded Boston, Roxbury, Mystic, Dorchester and Watertown, in an area called the Massachusetts Bay Colony.

1631 In the Thirty Years War, Catholic forces invaded the German Protestant town of Magdeburg, killed most of the population, and set fire to the place. The atrocity shocked Europe and led to demands for war to be fought according to an agreed set of rules.

1632 French settlers colonized eastern Canada and named it Acadia, now Nova Scotia.

◀ *Built as a flagship and equipped with superior firepower, Swedish king Gustavus II's two-decker* Vasa *sank as she embarked on her first voyage. After over 300 years, the ship was recovered and placed at the Vasa Ship Museum in Stockholm, Sweden.*

1632 In the Thirty Years War, Gustavus II Adolphus of Sweden defeated the Catholic League led by General von Tilly. Tilly died and Gustavas captured Munich. Swedish forces led by Gustavus II Adolphus defeated the Catholics in the Battle of Lützen, but Gustavus II Adolphus was killed.

1634 Poland and Russia called off their war with the Treaty of Polianov, according to which Russia gave up all the Polish territories that it had captured and Ladislas IV of Poland gave up his claim to the Russian throne.

1634 Kandahar was once again made part of the Mughal Empire when Shah Jahan defeated the Uzbeks of Central Asia and drove them out of Afghanistan.

1635 Saxony withdrew from the Thirty Years War after signing the Peace of Prague with the Holy Roman emperor Ferdinand II. However, the war continued between the Hapsburgs of Germany and the combined French and Swedish forces.

1636 Sugar cane was introduced in Barbados by a Dutch planter. It slowly replaced cotton, ginger, indigo and tobacco to become the chief crop of this Caribbean island.

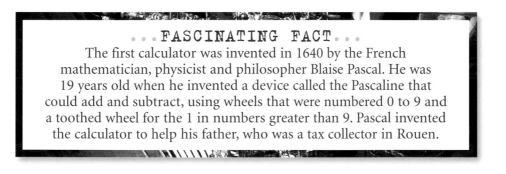

. . . . FASCINATING FACT . . . .
The first calculator was invented in 1640 by the French mathematician, physicist and philosopher Blaise Pascal. He was 19 years old when he invented a device called the Pascaline that could add and subtract, using wheels that were numbered 0 to 9 and a toothed wheel for the 1 in numbers greater than 9. Pascal invented the calculator to help his father, who was a tax collector in Rouen.

1636-1638

1636 The Japanese people were forbidden from travelling abroad by the country's shogun. This began an increasing policy of isolation by the Japanese that would last over 200 years.

1637 The French established trading posts along the Senegal River in Africa.

1637 The Dutch drove Portuguese colonists out of Costa Rica and established forts along the coast.

1637–1709 A series of weak rulers led to the decline of the Safavid dynasty. Its end came when the Ghalzai Afghans invaded Persia and occupied the city of Kandahar.

1637 North American tribesmen attacked and burned down the English town at Fort Mystic in Massachusetts.

1637 The first opera house, *Teatro San Cassiano*, opened in Venice. Most Venetian opera houses of the time were named after the nearest church. The *Teatro di San Cassiano* was no exception. As its popularity grew, the Venetian nobility rented the box seats, while the public was admitted to the lower-level seating at a cheaper price. The theatre was owned by the Tron family.

1638 Mauritius was colonized by the Dutch and named after John Maurice of Nassau, the Dutch governor in Brazil.

1638 Ottoman sultan Murad IV defeated the Persian Safavids and regained Baghdad. Murad IV ascended the throne after the dethronement of his insane uncle Mad Mustafa I. Over the next few years his mother Sultana Kösem ruled, but power was also held by the civil aristocracy and the military, who were mainly interested in their own advancement.

1638 Growing mistrust of the king, Charles I, and the increasing influence of his ideas on the Scottish Church caused the Scottish Presbyterians to protest.

▲ *Founded in 1636, Harvard University is the oldest American institution for higher education.*

1640-1646

1640 Portugal declared independence from Spain and elected João da Braganza as its ruler.

1641 The English Parliament had the Archbishop of Canterbury, William Laud, imprisoned for having used his power to harass and torture Presbyterians and Calvinsts.

1641 A peasant revolt in Ireland against their English landlords turned into a fight between the Catholics and Protestants, in which hundreds of Protestants lost their lives.

1641–1652 Buryat Mongols from Lake Baikal were defeated and brought under the control of the Russians.

1642 Tibet was formed as a religious state under the leadership of Ngawang Lobsang Gyatso, the fifth Dalai Lama.

1642 Dutch explorer Abel Janszoon Tasman discovered Tasmania . He went on to discover New Zealand.

▼ *The soldiers of the parliamentary side during the English Civil War were called Roundheads.*

1642 Civil war broke out in England. The issues were complex, but broadly the Anglican clergy, the landlords and the peasants supported Charles I, and the merchants, the noblemen and the middle classes supported Parliament.

1643 Louis XIII of France passed away and his son four-year-old son, Louis XIV, ascended the French throne. French forces defeated a combined force of Spanish, Dutch, Flemish and Italian soldiers in the Battle of Rocroi. France became the dominant military power in Europe.

▲ *English general Oliver Cromwell.*

1644 Manchurian invaders established the Ch'ing dynasty, the last great Chinese dynasty.

1646 Oliver Cromwell's parliamentary forces defeated the final army of Cavaliers, forcing King Charles I to surrender and put an end to the Civil War in England.

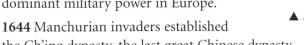

...FASCINATING FACT...
In the English Civil War the soldiers on the parliamentary side were called Roundheads. The name was used by those on the king's side to describe their Puritan rivals who had closely cropped hair, instead of the court fashion of long curly locks. The king's soldiers were called Cavaliers, which denoted brave knights on horseback. The royalists retained this name until 1679, when it was replaced by the term Tory.

1647-1651

1647 English clergyman George Fox, who was unhappy with Puritanism, founded a religious group called the 'Friends of Truth' at Leicestershire. The members of this group were later called the Quakers.

1648 The Peace of Westphalia ended the Eighty Years War between the Spaniards and the Dutch and the Thirty Years War between Germany, France and Sweden. A third of the population of Germany had died.

1648 Charles I was arrested by the English Parliament for having signed a secret treaty with the Scots. He was tried for treason against England, found guilty, and beheaded the following year. Following the execution of Charles I, England became a republic and Oliver Cromwell was made the Lord Protector of the Commonwealth. Oliver Cromwell came from a landowning class often called 'the gentry', which dominated the social and political life of the country. Until 1640, he played only a small role in local administration.

1648 The French nobility rose in revolt against Cardinal Mazarin, the prime minister of France. However, the uprising, which was called the Fronde, was badly organized and dragged on inconclusively for several years.

1649 Rebellions by Irish forces in Drogheda and Wexford were brutally put down by Oliver Cromwell.

1650 Following the arrest of the Great Condé, Duke of Beaufort and other Frondeurs, rebellion broke out in France, aided by an army from the Spanish Netherlands. However, the rebels were defeated in the Battle of Blanc-Champ.

▶ *Oliver Cromwell led the charge on the rebellious forces in the battle at Drogheda, Ireland. It was marked by large-scale massacre of the town's inhabitants, estimated at over 3000.*

1651 Charles II was crowned king of Scotland at
Scone in Scotland, and then marched into England
to claim the throne. He was defeated by Oliver
Cromwell in the Battle of Worcester. Charles was
forced to flee to France in disguise.

1651 Fort St James was built by the English
on the River Gambia to develop trade with
areas in the interior of western Africa.

1652-1660

1652 France was in political chaos due to the fight between the parliamentary Frondeurs led by the Great Condé and the royalists. The rebels entered Paris and established a government, but the peasants helped Louis XIV to enter the city and restore royal rule.

1653 The French Fronde was suppressed by the royalists and Cardinal Mazarin returned to Paris.

1654 Queen Christina of Sweden resigned from her post and joined the Catholic Church in Rome. She was succeeded by her cousin Charles X Gustavus. Earlier, in 1648, as commander of the Swedish army in Germany, Charles had participated in the last phase of the Thirty Years War.

1655 Charles X Gustavus of Sweden invaded Poland and captured Polish areas along the Baltic Sea.

1655 England occupied Jamaica to use it as a centre for their slave trade and as a base from where they could attack and raid Spanish colonies and ships.

◄ *Charles II claimed the crown of England after years of exile during the Puritan movement.*

1656 The first pendulum clock was invented by Christian Huygens, the Dutch mathematician-physicist. He was inspired by Galileo's study of pendulum movement in the cathedral of Pisa, famous for its leaning tower.

1657 Charles X Gustavus of Sweden invaded Denmark to increase his control over the Baltic coast, but he was defeated and driven out.

1658 Oliver Cromwell, the Lord Protector of the Commonwealth of England, Scotland and Ireland, died.

1658 Aurangzeb took over the Mughal throne and imprisoned his father Shah Jahan. He was a Sunni Muslim and did not tolerate other religions. Mughal literature and arts declined during his reign.

1660 Charles X Gustavus of Sweden died. He was succeeded by his son Charles XI. The new king ended Sweden's war with Denmark by signing the Treaty of Copenhagen and the Northern War against Poland with the Treaty of Oliva.

1660 Charles II became king of England after agreeing to accept concessions to Parliament. England returned to peace as a constitutional monarchy.

> ...**FASCINATING FACT**...
> As early as the 16th and 17th centuries, European fashion followed examples set by the French court. Styles popularized by Louis XIII and Louis XIV were adopted by all French subjects and even in England. Louis III could not grow a long beard, so he began the style of a small chin tuft. It soon became popular and replaced the long stiff beards that had previously been fashionable. Louis XIV used tall and elaborate wigs to increase his height and this too became fashionable, replacing the long natural locks both men and women used to wear earlier.

1661-1667

1661 Louis XIV gained complete control of France after the death of Cardinal Mazarin, his dominating prime minister.

1662 English scientist Robert Boyle formulated the famous Boyle's Law, which stated that the volume of a gas is inversely proportional to its pressure.

1664 England gained control of New Netherlands, which was renamed New York. English colonist Philip Carteret founded New Jersey and made Elizabethtown its capital.

1665 London was struck by its last big epidemic of plague, known as the Great Plague. About 15 percent of the population died.

1665 The second Anglo-Dutch war began when the Royal Navy defeated a Dutch fleet off Lowestoft.

1665 Philip IV, King of Spain, died. His young son ascended the Spanish throne as Charles II. The new king proved to be an ineffective ruler, he was the last Habsburg ruler of Spain.

1666 The city of London was destroyed in a great fire. The fire started in the house and shop of Thomas Farynor, King Charles II's baker in Pudding Lane. Farynor forgot to douse the fire in his oven and sparks that fell on the firewood stacked nearby caught flame. Three hours later, the house and shop were on fire. Farynor, his wife and daughter and one servant escaped by climbing through an upstairs window.

1666 English mathematician and Cambridge University professor Isaac Newton formulated calculus, a branch of mathematics used when the values being calculated keep varying. Calculus is used to solve engineering problems and astronomical calculations. The same year, he devised the law of gravity.

1667 Russia and Poland ended their war with the Treaty of Andrussovo, which gave Smolensk to Russia.

1667 The second Anglo-Dutch war ended with the Treaty of Breda.

▲ *The Great Fire of London is recorded as the worst fire in the city's history. The four-day blaze ravaged a large part of the city.*

1668-1676

▲ *In 1668, architect Louis Le Vau began to reconstruct the Palace of Versailles.*

1668 Poet, playwright and critic John Dryden became England's first literary personality to be honoured with the title of Poet Laureate.

1669 The Hanseatic League held its last meeting. This association of 150 trading cities collapsed due to internal disputes in Germany and rivalry from Britain and Holland.

1672 Puritans from Bermuda founded Charleston, South Carolina. It was named after Charles II, King of England.

1672 Ottoman Turks and Polish forces began a four-year war for the control of Ukraine, that was won by the Turks.

1673 Louis XIV of France was prevented from capturing Amsterdam when Dutch nobleman William III of Orange came to the rescue of the city.

1674 Following the death of the Polish king Michael Wisniowiecki, Poland's general John Sobieski ascended the throne. Sobieski defeated the Turkish army at Vienna, but his campaign for liberating Moldavia and Walachia from Turkish rule failed.

1675 Native tribes in New England led by King Philip – whose original name was Metacomet – raided 52 settlements and killed nearly 600 colonists in a revolt against being forced to pay an annual tribute (tax). The revolt was crushed, Philip executed and his people sold as slaves.

1675 Dutch microscopist Antonie van Leeuwenhoek became the first person to observe bacteria and protozoa with the help of his simple microscope. He also observed blood corpuscles, capillaries and the structure of nerves and muscles.

1676 The Observatory at Greenwich, England, was established to study the position of planets and develop a standard system of calculating time.

...FASCINATING FACT...

The Janissaries were a special army belonging to the Ottoman Turkish Empire. The members of this army were chosen at a young age from Christian families in the Balkans. Once chosen, they had to break ties with their families and undergo strict training. Their influence grew during the 15th and 16th centuries, and by the 17th century their power had increased so much that they practically controlled the Ottoman throne. In 1826 the Janissary army was wiped out when Sultan Mahmud II bombarded their barracks in Constantinople.

◄ *The sedan chair was carried on a pair of poles. In the 17th and 18th centuries, the sedan became an object of luxury in England, France and Italy.*

1678–1679 The Franco-Dutch war was ended by the signing of the Treaties of Nijmegen. The French agreed to suspend the anti-Dutch tariff of 1667 and to return Maastricht, but gained key fortresses on the border.

1680–1692 The Pueblos of New Mexico, North America, revolted and drove out 2500 Spanish colonists.

1680 Ietsuna, the Japanese Tokugawa shogun, died. He was succeeded by his brother Tsunayoshi, who promoted Neo-Confucianism in Japan. His reign is considered one of the most prosperous and peaceful periods in Japanese history.

1681 The Ch'ing dynasty under Emperor K'ang-hsi established control over the entire Chinese mainland by defeating the last three feudal states that had held out against them. K'ang-hsi also checked Russian expansion by signing the Treaty of Nerchinsk.

1681 Tartar provinces beside the Volga River were captured by the Russians and their inhabitants were forcibly converted to Christianity.

1681 Louis XIV moved the French court to the grand palace he had built in Versailles. The move completed the process begun by Louis XIII in 1624 which gave absolute power to the king. Nobles had to live at Versailles in return for position and wealth, so the king could control them.

1682 Austria and Poland went to war against the Ottoman Turks to free Hungary from their control.

1682 Peter I, also known as Peter the Great, was crowned the joint Tsar of Russia with his 16-year-old brother, Ivan. As Peter was only nine years old, his 25-year-old sister Sophia became regent for the brothers and ruled on their behalf.

1683 Spain and the Holy Roman emperor Leopold I joined Holland and Sweden in their war against Louis XIV.

...FASCINATING FACT...

Manchu women celebrated New Year's Eve by going for walks with groups of friends. The ritual of 'walking away sickness' was done in the belief that this could prevent illness in the New Year. The walk was also an opportunity to show off their new clothes and beautifully embroidered shoes. The silk shoes were stitched on to wooden platforms to prevent them from getting dirty.

1683–1690

1683 An Ottoman attack on Vienna failed due to German and Polish troops coming to the aid of the city. Viennese bakers invented a new pastry to celebrate: the croissant.

1684 The English East India Company established their first trading post in China at Canton, after having traded in Chinese goods for nearly 80 years through Java.

1685 Louis XIV of France issued the Edict of Fontainebleau, which cancelled the Edict of Nantes. The new edict ordered the destruction of Huguenot Churches and closing of Protestant schools. More than 50,000 French Huguenot families left France and settled in Holland, South Africa, North America, Denmark, the Protestant German states and England. The economic dislocation this caused in France badly affected government finances.

1685 James, duke of Monmouth, laid claim to the English throne against his Catholic uncle James II. Teh rebellion failed and Monmouth was executed.

1686 In India, the city of Calcutta (now Kolkata) was founded by Job Charnock, an administrator in the East India Company.

1687 Charles of Lorraine defeated the Ottoman Turks in the second Battle of Mohács. This victory allowed Leopold I of Austria to take over Hungary, a kingdom his family had inherited 150 years earlier.

1688 England's 'Glorious Revolution' led to the removal of James II from power. The move replaced Roman Catholic rule in England with Protestant rule when they invited James' daughter Mary and her husband William of Orange to occupy the English throne. The new monarchs introduced important democratic reforms.

1689 William and Mary of England were invited to accept the Scottish throne. The Jacobite party revolted against the new king under the leadership of the Viscount of Dundee, who wanted to see the exiled James II restored to the throne. The Jacobite threat ended with the death of Dundee.

1690 William III of England landed in Ireland and defeated the exiled James II in the Battle of the Boyne, forcing him to flee the country.

1690 Bulgaria, Serbia, Transylvania and Belgrade were recaptured by the Ottoman Turks from the Austrians.

◀ *Mary II and her Dutch husband, William III.*

115

1692–1698

1692–1693 Spanish forces suppressed the Native Americans of the New Mexican pueblos and took control of the area once again.

1693 French naval forces defeated an Anglo-Dutch fleet off Cape St Vincent and defeated a British fleet in the Battle of Lagos.

1694 The Bank of England was established in London and was given the status of the most important financial institution in England. Often called the 'old lady of Threadneedle Street', the bank started with a capital of 12 million pounds. In exchange for the loan of its entire capital to the government, the bank received the right to issue notes and a monopoly on corporate banking in England. The bank introduced reforms that gave England the world's first modern finance sytem, and thus was more stable than most others.

1694–1778 French writer Francois Voltaire lived during this period. He is considered to be one of the greatest French writers. *Candide* is his best-known work.

1696 John III Sobieski, King of Poland, died. Frederick of Saxony was elected to the Polish throne. He assumed the name of Augustus II and ruled for 37 years. During his reign, Poland declined from being a major European power to a protectorate of Russia.

1697 Charles XI of Sweden died. His son Charles XII succeeded him. He promoted important domestic reforms. His disastrous invasion of Russia, however, marked the end of Sweden's status as a major power.

1697 The Ottoman Turks, led by Sultan Mustafa II, faced a crushing defeat in the Battle of Zenta against Austria. This victory made Austria the leading power in central Europe.

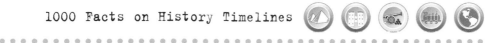

▲ The London Stock Exchange was established in
1698 and became a public limited company in 1991.

1698 The London Stock Exchange was established. Although other European
cities like Antwerp had organized trading houses, the exchange at London was
the first of its kind in the world.

1698 The first steam engine was designed and made by English engineer
Thomas Savery. The engine was made to pump out water from coal mines,
though the idea was later adapted to other purposes.

1699–1711

1699 In India, Sikh leader Guru Gobind Singh formed the Sikh army, the Khalsa, to protect Sikhs from Mughal emperor Aurangazeb's cruelty. The Mughal Empire was weakened by continuous rebellions.

1699 English adventurer and explorer William Dampier explored the west coast of Australia and discovered the Pacific island of New Britain.

1700 Carlos II died in Spain without leaving any children. The throne was claimed by Frenchman Philip of Anjou, Charles of Austria and Joseph of Bavaria. The War of the Spanish Succession between the three men divided Europe and lasted for 11 years. England, Denmark and the Holy Roman emperor Leopold I opposed the succession of Philip. They formed the Grand Alliance and invaded France.

1701 Frederick I, elector of Brandenburg, enlarged his territories and obtained a treaty from Emperor Leopold I that promoted him to the position of king of Prussia.

1701 English agriculturist and inventor Jethro Tull revolutionized farming by the invention of the horse-drawn hoe and seeding drill. He also stressed the use of manure and the importance of breaking up the soil into small pieces.

1703 Peter the Great, tsar of Russia, founded the fort at the city of St Petersburg. The city remained the capital of Russia for two centuries.

1706 In the War of the Spanish Succession, forces led by the Duke of Marlborough defeated the French in the Battle of Ramillies and occupied the Spanish Netherlands.

1709 Englishman Abraham Darby discovered that iron ore could be smelted using coke, to produce pig iron. Coke proved superior to charcoal by allowing larger furnaces and being much cheaper. The iron from his establishment was later used for building a cast-iron bridge and for the first locomotive with a high-pressure boiler. Iron became much cheaper to produce and became a key factor in the Industrial Revolution.

1711 The War of the Spanish Succession saw all sides exhausted by the fighting and peace talks began.

▼ *Jethro Tull's inventions, such as the horse-drawn hoe, laid the foundation for efficient and scientific farming.*

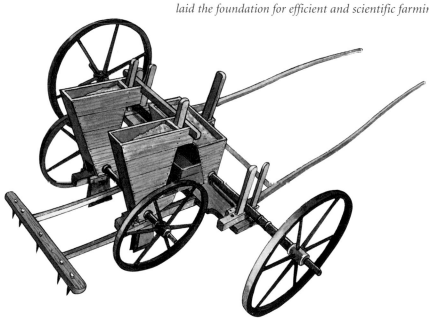

1712-1725

◀ *The celebrated* Gulliver's Travels *by Jonathan Swift (1667–1745) depicted the voyages of its hero, set amid fantastical settings. It is regarded as a masterpiece of parody.*

1712 Swiss-French philosopher Jean-Jacques Rousseau was born. His *Confessions* is his famous autobiography.

1714 The War of the Spanish Succession and the Queen Anne's War were ended with the Peace of Utrecht. France signed treaties with Britain, Prussia, the Dutch Republic, Portugal and Savoy, and was forced to surrender several territories, including some in Canada, to Britain. France also recognized Queen Anne of Britain, Frederick I and Victor Amadeus II of Sicily. Spain gave Gibraltar to Britain and also gave the British the exclusive right to supply African slaves in Spanish colonies for 30 years.

1714 The mercury thermometer was invented by the German physicist Daniel Gabriel Fahrenheit.

1714 Queen Anne of England died. George I, elector of Hanover and grandson of James I, was crowned king of England, Scotland and Ireland. The Jacobite Revolt, led by the earl of Mar, aimed to put the exiled James III, the Old Pretender, on the throne of Britain, instead of George I. It was suppressed in the Battle of Sheriff Muir. This revolt became known as 'The 15'.

1719–1748 During the reign of Mughal emperor Muhammad Shah, the empire lost its power as local rulers became more independent. However, art and architecture flourished under his patronage.

1722 The Safavid capital Isfahan was captured by the Ghazlai Afghans and Iran was thrown into chaos following the defeat of the Safavids. The unstable conditions of the country led to the loss of Darba and Baku to the Russians, and Azerbaijan to the Ottoman Turks.

1723–1790 Scottish philosopher and economist Adam Smith's lived during this period. He was the author of *An Inquiry into the Nature and Causes of the Wealth of Nations*, an important work in the field of economics.

1725 Tahmasp II Safavi regained the Persian throne with the help of Nadir Quli of the Afshar tribe, who also helped him regain the territories lost to the Russians and the Turks.

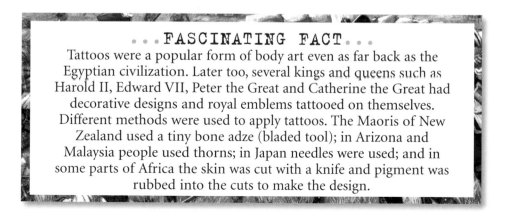

...FASCINATING FACT...
Tattoos were a popular form of body art even as far back as the Egyptian civilization. Later too, several kings and queens such as Harold II, Edward VII, Peter the Great and Catherine the Great had decorative designs and royal emblems tattooed on themselves. Different methods were used to apply tattoos. The Maoris of New Zealand used a tiny bone adze (bladed tool); in Arizona and Malaysia people used thorns; in Japan needles were used; and in some parts of Africa the skin was cut with a knife and pigment was rubbed into the cuts to make the design.

1735-1749

1735 Englishman John Harrison invented the chronometer, a device used by navigators to measure time and longitude.

1736 Nadir Quli ascended the Persian throne after the death of Abbas III and established the Afsharid dynasty, taking on the title Nadir Shah. He looted Delhi , carrying off the famed Peacock Throne (studded with gold and gems) and the Kohinoor Diamond.

▲ *Maria Theresa played a key role in the political affairs of Europe in the 18th century.*

1740 Maria Theresa, daughter of the late Holy Roman emperor Charles VI, was made archduchess of Austria and queen of Hungary and Bohemia. This sparked the Austrian War of Succession when Charles VII of Bavaria claimed the Austrian crown, invaded Bohemia and captured Prague.

1741 Muhammad ibn 'Abd-al-Wahhab, founder of the Islamic Wahhabi sect, combined forces with local chieftain Muhammad ibn Sa'ud to conquer the Arabian Peninsula, establish the Sa'udi dynasty and spread the Wahhabi faith.

1745 Combined Dutch, British and Hanoverian forces, led by the duke of Cumberland, were defeated by the French in the Battle of Fontenoy. Britain withdrew from the Austrian War of Succession.

1745 Francis I, husband of Maria Theresa of Austria, was elected the Holy Roman Emperor.

1745 Charles Edward Stuart, also known as Bonnie Prince Charlie, led the second Jacobite revolt. Although successful in capturing the English towns of Carlisle, Preston and Manchester, he was defeated in the Battle of Culloden.

1748 The Treaty of Aix-la-Chapelle ended the War of the Austrian Succession. France gained Louisbourg in Nova Scotia, while Madras, in India, went to Britain. The treaty gave Maria Theresa the Austrian lands.

1749–1832 Johann Wolfgang von Goethe lived during this period. He was one of Germany's most outstanding writers. *The Sorrows of Young Werther*, *The Elf King* and *Faust* are some of his best known works.

▼ *The Battle of Culloden, which lasted only about 40 minutes, was a decisive reverse for the Jacobites led by Charles Edward.*

1756–1762

1756 Maria Theresa of Austria formed an alliance with France, Russia and Saxony against Prussia. Frederick II of Prussia captured Saxony and began the Seven Years War.

1756–1791 Austrian composer Wolfgang Amadeus Mozart lived during this period. He is considered one of the greatest composers of all times.

1757 In India, Bengal came under British rule when forces of the East India Company, led by Robert Clive, defeated Siraj ud-Daula, the Nawab of Bengal, in the Battle of Plassey. The British had 3000 troops, while the nawab had 50,000 men. The British won the battle with their superior artillery and because Clive had bribed Mir Jaffer, the general of the nawab.

1757 Frederick II of Prussia defeated the Austrians in the Battle of Leuthen. The Prussian army comprised 39,000 men and 167 cannons, while the Austrians had 58,500 men and 210 cannons.

1758 In the French and Indian War, the British colonial forces defeated the French at Louisborg in Canada. The following year, British colonial forces led by James Wolfe defeated the French and captured Quebec in the Battle of the Plains of Abraham.

1760 King George III became the king of Great Britain and Ireland. His efforts to raise funds through taxation of the American colonies would later lead to the American Revolution.

1761 The Bridgewater Canal was constructed to carry coal from Worsley to Manchester. It was later extended to Mersey, putting Liverpool on the canal route. This was the world's first entirely artificial waterway.

▶ *The Battle of Plassey set the stage for establishing British rule in India. The British forces won the day despite being vastly outnumbered.*

1762 Following the death of the Russian empress Elizabeth, her son Peter III ascended the throne, but he was unpopular. He was forced by the nobles of Russia to make way for his wife Catherine II, also known as Catherine the Great. She reorganized administration and law and expanded Russian territory.

1763 After several victories and losses on both sides, Prussia won the Seven Years War, which ended with the Treaty of Hubertusburg, establishing Prussia as a major European power.

1763-1775

1763 North American tribes destroyed several British forts near Niagara, and surrounded the British colony at Detroit, attacking the inhabitants. The Native Americans were defeated near Pittsburgh.

1764 Scottish inventor James Watt designed his first steam engine. He spent the next 30 years improving his design to make steam engines far more powerful and reliable.

1765 Joseph II succeeded his father Francis I as the Holy Roman emperor. He abolished serfdom, established religious equality before the law, and granted freedom to the press. Joseph angered the Roman Catholic Church by attempting to impose state control over it.

1767 English inventor James Hargreaves developed a hand-operated spinning machine, the spinning jenny, which increased the amount of thread produced. It is one of the first mass-production industrial machines.

◀ *James Watt's steam engine vastly improved upon the efficiency of the device built earlier by Newcomen. The Watt engine began to be used – in mills and canals, and later in steamboats and locomotives.*

1767 The Burmese captured Ayudhya, forcing the Thai royal family to flee to Cambodia.

1768 English naval captain and explorer James Cook set out on the first of his Pacific expeditions, during which he visited New Zealand and discovered the Great Barrier Reef off Australia.

1769 Sir Richard Arkwright invented the 'water frame' to spin stronger cotton yarn. Arkwright later installed water frames at Crompton Mill, Derby, making it the world's first industrial factory.

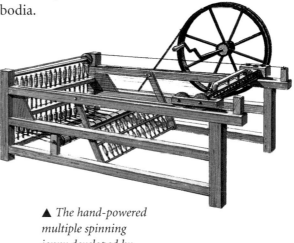

▲ *The hand-powered multiple spinning jenny developed by James Hargreaves.*

1770–1827 German Classical composer Ludwig van Beethoven lived during this period.

1774 The British Parliament passed a number of acts called the Coercive Acts. They restricted the freedom of American colonies and increased Britain's domination over them.

1775 George Washington was appointed the general and commander-in-chief of the Continental Army, the joint army of the British colonies in North America.

1775 French scholar and philosopher Denis Diderot completed his *Encyclopedia*, which reflected his views on philosophy and science.

127

1775-1778

1775 The American War of Independence began with a fight between the British forces and the local militia at Concord in Massachusetts.

1775 British troops captured military stores at Lexington. Two months later, 15,000 colonial troops assembled near Bunker Hill in Boston to prevent the British from occupying that area. However, the colonists were eventually forced to retreat. The British suffered about 1000 casualties.

1776 The viceroyalty of La Plata was established in Spanish South America, and Buenos Aires was made its capital.

1776 The Declaration of American Independence, drafted by Thomas Jefferson and others, was approved by the Congress. The document announced the separation of 13 North American colonies from Britain.

1776 British naval explorer Captain James Cook set out on his third and final voyage in search of a northwestern passage around Canada. The expedition was unsuccessful and Cook was killed by the natives of Hawaii.

1776 George Washington's American army defeated British forces in the Battle of Harlem Heights, New York.

1777 The industrial centres of the English Midlands was connected to the ports at Hull, Liverpool and Bristol by the Grand Trunk Canal.

1777 The United States Congress adopted the United States flag, which had 13 stars and 13 stripes in red and white.

1777 American troops had their first major victory against the British in the Battles of Saratoga.

1778 America signed treaties with France, in which France recognized the independence of the United States and assured military support in their war against England. Spain joined the fight on America's side the following year.

◀ *The national flag of the United States features 50 stars representing the 50 states and 13 stripes for the original 13 states.*

1778-1788

1778–1829 British chemist Sir Humphry Davy lived during this period. Davy made significant discoveries in chemistry and experimented with electricity.

1779 Englishman Samuel Crompton invented the spinning mule, a completely automated spinning machine that produced yarn in bulk.

1780 Peruvian Indian nobility lost their power and wealth due to the harsh steps taken by the Spanish government to put down a revolt led by Tupac Amaru II. Native governors were appointed to maintain law and order.

1781 British naval forces were defeated by a French fleet just off Yorktown in South Carolina, after which the American army led by George Washington forced General Cornwallis and his troops to surrender Yorktown.

1783 The Treaty of Paris was signed by the United States and Great Britain, concluding the American Revolution. Britain recognized the independence of 13 colonies in North America.

1783 Shahin Girai, ruler of Crimea and the last descendant of Genghis Khan, was defeated by Catherine the Great of Russia and Crimea became part of the Russian Empire.

1783 British industrialist Henry Cort developed a method called the 'puddling' process by which pig iron could be converted into wrought iron. He also obtained a patent for producing iron bars economically and quickly in a rolling mill with grooved rolls. His inventions provided a major boost to the British iron-making industry and iron production increased significantly.

1783 French brothers Joseph-Michel Montgolfier and Jacques-Étienne Montgolfier developed the first hot-air balloon, which rose to a height of 1000 m and remained aloft for ten minutes. Next, they sent a sheep, a rooster and a duck as passengers. The first manned flight took place on November 21.

1784 The first Russian settlement in America was founded on Kodiak Island in Alaska.

1785 Aqa Muhammad Khan of the Qajar tribe in Persia took control of the northern provinces, declared himself shah and established his capital at Tehran. Over the next 15 years, he brought all of Iran under his control.

1788 British naval captain Arthur Philip arrived with the First Fleet at Botany Bay and established the convict colony of New South Wales, the first European settlement in Australia.

◀ *The Montgolfier brothers devised the first hot-air balloon. They burnt straw and wool beneath the balloon to fill it with heated air.*

131

1789–1793

◀ *The cornerstone of the Capitol, seat of the Congress in Washington, DC, was laid by George Washington on September 18, 1793.*

1789 Unhappy with the monarchy, the poverty and the unequal class system in France, the middle class elected radical reformers to the National Assembly.

1789 King Louis XVI of France called French troops to surround Paris and Versailles, and sacked the prime minister Jacques Necker. Frenzied mobs demonstrated in front of the palace and broke into the Bastille, a prison in Paris.

1789 The French National Assembly made Marquis de Lafayette commander of the National Guards and Jean-Sylvain Bailly the Mayor of Paris. The 'Declaration of the Rights of Man and of the Citizen' was made by the National Assembly to set out equal rights to all Frenchmen. Many areas of France collapsed into violent anarchy.

1789 George Washington and John Adams were elected the first president and vice president, respectively, of the United States by the House of Representatives and the Senate.

1791 Louis XVI tried to flee France with his family, but he was caught at Varennes and imprisoned.

1791 James Hoban was commissioned to build the White House in Washington, DC, the official residence of the president of the United States.

1792 France declared war against Prussia and Austria following their attempts to interfere in the French Revolution. After several initial defeats, French forces defeated the Prussians at Valmy. The French National Assembly then dethroned Louis XVI and declared a republic. Dozens of noblemen were convicted of opposing the new regime and executed.

1793 Louis XVI of France and his wife Marie Antoinette were accused of betraying the new French Republic. They were found guilty and executed. The Reign of Terror that followed saw thousands declared enemies of the Revolution and executed.

1793 Poland was partitioned, with extensive border areas going to Russia and Prussia.

...**FASCINATING FACT**...
The guillotine was first used for execution in France in 1792. Joseph-Ignace Guillotin, a doctor and a member of the National Assembly, said that sentences of death should be carried out by a machine, so that death by beheading would not be confined to nobles and executions would be as painless as possible. The last execution was in 1977, after which France abolished capital punishment.

1794 In France, Maximilien Robespierre, the Jacobin leader behind the Reign of Terror, was executed. Civil war and revolts continued in France.

1795 Russia and Prussia put down a Polish revolt against the partitioning of their country. The remaining parts of Poland were then divided between Russia and Prussia.

1796 British surgeon Edward Jenner developed the vaccine against smallpox. He showed that people who contracted the relatively harmless disease, cowpox, became immune to smallpox.

1797–1860 Christian missionaries in Polynesia destroyed the religious idols of the natives and persuaded them to convert to Christianity.

1797 Aqa Muhammad Khan, shah of Persia, was killed. He was succeeded by his nephew Fath Ali Shah. The new king quelled a rebellion in Khorasan, but failed to defeat the European powers. He also warred against Russia.

1798 In Ireland there was an unsuccessful rebellion against the British.

1799 The Directorate of France was forced to resign and the Consulate was established with successful general Napoleon Bonaparte as First Consul. The new government was effectively a military dictatorship.

▶ *The 18th-century French Revolution lasted over a decade.*

1800 Bone china was invented by the British potter Josiah Spode.

1801 The Act of Union was passed, which united Great Britain and Ireland under the name of the United Kingdom. The flag created by the merger, the Union Flag (or Jack), still remains the flag of the United Kingdom. The upright red cross on the flag represents England. The blue background represents Scotland, while the diagonal red cross represents Ireland.

1802 The British crown won complete control over Sri Lanka by the Treaty of Amiens, which was signed by Britain, France, Spain and Batavia during the Napoleonic Wars.

1803 The United States of America bought Louisiana from the French for $15 million. Louisiana covered all North America west of the Mississippi River to the Rocky Mountains. The 'Louisiana Purchase' doubled the area of the USA.

1803 British engineer Richard Trevithick invented the first high-pressure railway steam engine. He later modified his engine to be used in an iron-rolling mill and to power a barge.

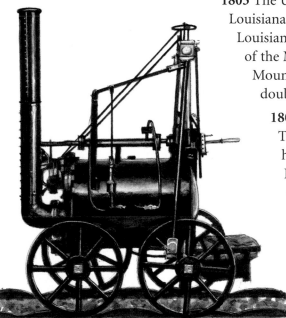

◄ *Richard Trevithick's steam locomotive had its first run in 1804, hauling 10 tonnes of iron and 70 men along a 17-km stretch.*

1804-1812

1804 Napoleon Bonaparte became emperor of France. Earlier, in 1802, Napoleon had instituted a new constitution whereby he secured the position of First Consul for life.

1804–1830 The Black War was fought between the Aborigines of Tasmania and European settlers and soldiers. Most of the Aborigines were killed by the war's end.

1805 Napoleon's French troops defeated Russia and Austria in the Battle of Austerlitz. Meanwhile, a British fleet led by Admiral Horatio Nelson defeated a fleet of French and Spanish ships in the Battle of Trafalgar, ending Napoleon's ambition of invading England.

◄ *Lord Nelson's full title at the time of his death was Vice Admiral of the White The Right Honourable Horatio, Viscount Nelson, Knight of the Most Honourable Order of Bath.*

1807 American engineer and inventor Robert Fulton designed the first commercially successful steamship *Clermont*. The boat sailed between New York and Albany, completing the 240-km journey in 32 hours. Fulton later designed several other steamboats, including the world's first steam warship.

1809 France defeated Austria in the Battle of Wagram. In this battle, 154,000 French troops led by Napoleon fought against 158,000 Austrian troops led by Archduke Charles. The attack of the French forces forced the Austrians to retreat. About 40,000 Austrians and 34,000 French died.

1809–1882 British naturalist Charles Darwin lived during this time. His research and writings contributed greatly to the understanding of the evolution of life forms. He wrote *On the Origin of Species by Means of Natural Selection* based on his theory.

1812 Emperor Napoleon invaded Russia and defeated the Russians in the Battle of Borodino. Napoleon captured Moscow but was soon forced to retreat.

1812 United States went to war against Britain due to the latter's unfair maritime practices. The war ended two years later with the Treaty of Ghent.

1812–1870 British author Charles Dickens lived during this time. *David Copperfield*, *A Tale of Two Cities* and *Great Expectations* are some of his most famous works and are considered to be English classics.

1814-1821

▲ *The Battle of Waterloo was the last battle of Napoleon Bonaparte.*

1814 Paris was invaded by European allies and Emperor Napoleon was defeated and exiled to Elba. The Bourbon dynasty came back to power in France with King Louis XVIII.

1814–1838 Christian missionaries arrived in New Zealand. They were soon followed by European traders.

1815 Napoleon returned to France and raised a new army, but was defeated in the Battle of Waterloo by a British army under the Duke of Wellington, aided by the Prussians. Napoleon was exiled to the island of St Helena.

1816 Argentina declared its independence from Spain, and named itself the United Provinces of the Río de la Plata. Chilean revolutionaries led by Bernardo O'Higgins defeated the Spanish forces ruling Chile. O'Higgins became the supreme director of Chile.

1817–1818 The First Seminole War was fought between United States troops and the Seminole tribe of Florida. In 1818, 3000 United States soldiers led by Major General Andrew Jackson attacked. The Seminole were defeated and agreed to allow free use of Seminole lands by American settlers.

1818 The British East India Company established control over much of India.

1818–1823 German historian and economist Karl Marx lived during this time. He wrote *Communist Manifesto* and *Das Kapital*, which were the basis of Marxism (the foundation of Socialism and Communism).

1819 An expedition of the East India Company, headed by Sir Stamford Raffles, established itself in Singapore.

▲ *Karl Marx spent much of his life in poverty, supported by his friends. He established the philosophical basis of later Communist movements.*

1821 The Treaty of Córdoba was signed, giving Mexico independence from Spain.

1821 The Gold Coast in Africa became a British colony.

1821 Argentinian General José de San Martín drove out the Spanish rulers of Peru and liberated the country.

1821 The Ottoman Turks defeated the Greek revolutionary forces in the Battle of Dragasani. The Greeks continued their campaign for independence.

1824 Frenchman Louis Braille invented Braille, a writing system using raised dots to enable blind people to read. The Braille code for English was adopted in 1932.

1825 In South America, Bolivia gained independence and Antonio José de Sucre became its first president in the following year.

1825 British engineer and inventor George Stephenson made a steam-powered locomotive for the first passenger railway, between Stockton and Darlington in England. The train could carry 450 passengers.

1826–1827 Frenchman Nicéphore Niepce produced the first permanent photograph using a technique he called heliography.

◀ *The use of steam power in ships became a practical idea after James Watt's success with his steam engine.*

1827 A fleet of British, French and Russian ships destroyed a Turko-Egyptian fleet in the Battle of Navarino. The superior guns of the European fleet destroyed three-quarters of the Turko-Egyptian fleet. This was the last significant battle between wooden ships and led to the expulsion of Greece from Turkey.

1828 Russia invaded Persia and defeated the Persian forces, forcing them to sign the Treaty of Turkmanchai, whereby Russia got all Persian lands north of the Caspian Sea. Russia also invaded Anatolia, defeated the Turks and forced them to sign the Treaty of Edirne, whereby Russia got the eastern shore of the Black Sea, Georgia and parts of Armenia.

1828–1910 Russian novelist Leo Tolstoy lived during this period. *War and Peace* and *Anna Karenina* are two of his best known works.

1829 The British colony of Western Australia was established. The first group of settlers who arrived there were led by Captain James Stirling. This was Australia's first non-convict colony. In 1886, gold was discovered in Western Australia and constitutional autonomy was granted by the British in 1890.

1830 France invaded Algeria, swiftly suppressing Algerian forces and occupying the African kingdom. By 1847, the French had established military control in Algeria and were successful in establishing civil rule in the late 19th century. Areas of the interior mountains remained defiant and resisted French rule.

1830 Belgium won its independence from the Netherlands, and Brussels was made its capital. Leopold I was chosen as king by the Belgian National Congress.

1830 The Mormon sect was founded by Joseph Smith in New York.

1831 British scientist and inventor Michael Faraday published his findings regarding the generation of electricity through electromagnetic induction.

1832 The Egyptian ruler Muhammad Ali defeated the Ottoman army in the Battle of Konya, in central Anatolia. Earlier that year, Ali had captured Damascus in Syria from Sultan Mahmud II.

1833 The Slavery Abolition Act was passed by the British parliament, granting all slaves in the British Empire their freedom.

1835–1840 The Boers of South Africa began a mass migration, 'The Great Trek', from the British-controlled lands to Transvaal and the Orange River.

▲ *Michael Faraday, known for designing ingenious experiments, was largely self-educated.*

1836 Texas declared its independence from Mexico. Alamo, in San Antonio, Texas, was besieged by Mexican forces. Under 200 men defended the fort against 3000 Mexican troops for 13 days before the fort was captured.

1837–1839 Members of the British working class launched the Chartist Movement, named after the People's Charter of 1838. They demanded equal rights and participation in parliamentary elections.

1838 American inventor Samuel J Morse invented Morse Code. In this system, letters, numbers and punctuation marks are represented by a sequence of dots, dashes and spaces. Signals can be sent as electrical impulses, mechanical or visual signals.

1839 British blacksmith Kirkpatrick Macmillan invented the first practical bicycle. His machine was propelled by pedals, cranks and drive rods.

1839–1842 Britain defeated China in the Opium War and made China sign the Treaty of Nanking. Britain was given Hong Kong and the British traders were given greater privileges.

...FASCINATING FACT...

In the 1830s, British mathematician and inventor Charles Babbage began developing the Analytical Engine, a digital computer. His work drew a lot of attention and one of the people interested in it was the Countess of Lovelace, Ada Augusta King. Lady Lovelace, who was a mathematician, created a programme for the Analytical Engine. Unfortunately, the first computer program ever written was never used because Babbage never completed his computing device!

1840–1848

1840 British educator Rowland Hill organized the modern postal system in Britain, devising the first pre-paid postage stamp.

1840–1926 French painter Claude Monet lived during this period. He was one of the most important artists of the Impressionist style.

1842 American physician John Gorrie invented a system of refrigeration and air-cooling through experiments conducted to provide air-conditioned rooms for patients suffering from fever.

1843 In the Battle of Miani, Sindh was conquered by the British in India and brought under the Bombay Presidency.

1845 In India, the Sikh kingdom of Punjab was defeated by British forces at Sobraon and forced to sign the Treaty of Lahore – Kashmir and Jalandhar went to the British. Kashmir was later sold to Gulab Singh, ruler of Jammu.

1845 Texas became part of the United States.

1845–1849 Ireland suffered the Great Potato Famine when entire crops of potato, the staple Irish food, were ruined. The famine was a consequence of the appearance of blight, the potato fungus. About 800,000 people died as a result of the famine. A large number of people migrated to Britain, the United States, Canada and Australia.

> ### . . . FASCINATING FACT . . .
> The world's first postage stamp, the Penny Black, a one-penny stamp with Queen Victoria's profile against a black background was produced in 1840. It was used for letters weighing less than half an ounce. For heavier letters the Twopenny Blue was used, which was similar, except that its background was blue.

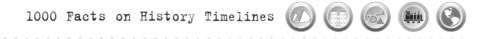

▲ *British officials were sent to govern India during what is now called the Raj – the period of British imperial rule in India.*

1846–1848 In the Mexican War, United States forces defeated the Mexicans and occupied Mexico City. Under the Treaty of Guadalupe Hidalgo, the United States bought New Mexico, Utah, Nevada, Arizona, California, Texas and Colorado for 15 million dollars.

1848 A series of revolutions started in various parts of Europe, beginning with Sicily, and spreading to France, Germany and Austria. They were mostly unsuccessful in bringing about any political change, and were all eventually suppressed.

145

1852–1861

1852 Napoleon III, the grandson of Napoleon I, was elected to be the emperor of France. During his reign, craftsmen formed associations to get finance for insurance.

1852 In the Second Anglo-Burmese War, British forces captured Lower Burma. While the war ended in British victory, it proved expensive for the East India Company, costing them one million pounds and making them unpopular with those in India who had to pay the bill.

1853 Japan and the United States signed the Kanagawa Treaty, allowing the United States to establish a base in Japan and conduct trade. It was the first treaty that Japan signed with a Western country and was forced on Japan by American warships.

1853 The Crimean War was fought between Russia and an alliance comprising the Ottoman Empire, the kingdom of Sardinia, Britain and France. The war is best known for the almost suicidal charge of the Light Brigade of British cavalry. The Crimean War ended with the Treaty of Paris which limited Russian power in the Black Sea area.

1854 The Suez Canal in Egypt was opened, connecting the Mediterranean Sea with the Red Sea.

1856–1939 Austrian neurologist Sigmund Freud lived during this period. His path-breaking work led to the development of psychoanalysis.

1857–1858 The Sepoy Mutiny among Indian troops in British service spread rapidly to military stations all over northern and western India. It was eventually suppressed by British troops. The British Parliament passed the Government of India Act, ending the rule of the East India Company and bringing India under British rule.

1859 The Maoris of New Zealand clashed violently with European settlers, heralding the beginning of the second Maori Wars.

1860 The Confederate States of America was formed when 11 southern states broke away from the United States. Jefferson Davis was elected the Confederacy president. The 11 states of the Confederacy were North Carolina, South Carolina, Florida, Alabama, Georgia, Arkansas, Mississippi, Louisiana, Tennessee, Virginia and Texas.

1861 Victor Emmanuel II became the first king of Italy. The capital city changed from Turin to Florence, and in 1870, Emmanuel II made Rome the official capital of Italy.

▼ *The 1857 Sepoy Mutiny in India began in Meerut and then spread to Delhi, Agra, Kanpur and Lucknow.*

1861–1867

1861 Republican Abraham Lincoln was sworn in as the 16th president of the United States. Before he entered politics, Lincoln worked as a rail-splitter, a lawyer and a store clerk!

1861 The American Civil War began, with the Confederates making their first attack on Fort Sumter in South Carolina.

1862 Confederate forces led by Robert E Lee defeated the Union Army in the Seven Days' Battle. Also known as the Seven Days Campaign, the week-long battle ended after Lee forced General McClellan and his Army of the Potomac to retreat.

1863 President Lincoln made his Emancipation Proclamation, promising to free all slaves in the Confederate states. The document officially banned slavery in the country, and also allowed slaves to join the military forces.

1863 The Battle of Gettysburg was fought between the Confederates and Union forces. After the loss of nearly 20,000 lives on both sides, the Confederates withdrew.

▲ *Lincoln's Gettysburg Address is one of the most famous speeches ever delivered in the United States.*

1863 In the American Civil War, Vicksburg was captured by Union forces, dividing the Confederate states in two.

1864 Denmark was defeated by the combined forces of Prussia and Austria, and was forced to give up the provinces of Schleswig and Holstein to joint Prussian-Austrian control.

1865 Ulysses S Grant, commander of the Union forces, captured Richmond and forced Confederate general Robert E Lee to surrender. The American Civil War ended with the Confederate states being forced to rejoin the United States.

1866 In the Seven Weeks War, Prussia defeated the combined forces of Austria, Hanover, Saxony, Bavaria and some minor German states, and established itself as the leader of German states. The German Confederation was formed with Berlin as its capital.

1867 Russia sold Alaska to the United States for over seven million dollars.

▼ *The Vicksburg Campaign allowed the Union forces to cut off the Confederate states located west of the Mississippi River, from those that lay to the east.*

1868–1885

1868 The Tokugawa shogunate in Japan came to an end after a political revolution called the Meiji Restoration. Subsequently, Emperor Meiji ascended the throne as the first modern emperor of Japan, ruling the country himself instead of through a military shogun.

1868 Isabella II, Queen of Spain, was forced to flee the country due to a revolution led by democrats and powerful and wealthy rebels who wanted to establish themselves in the Spanish government.

1869 The Suez Canal, which connected the Red Sea with the eastern Mediterranean Sea, was opened.

1870 German states led by Prussia defeated France in the Franco-Prussian War. Victory signified the end of the domination of France in Europe, and marked the beginning of a unified Germany under the leadership of Prussia. Napoleon III of France stepped down from the throne after losing the Franco-Prussian War, and the Third French Republic was established.

1872 The Yellowstone National Park in the United States was established, giving the world its first national park.

1876 Scottish-born American inventor Alexander Graham Bell invented the telephone. Bell later went on to establish the Bell Telephone Company.

> ...**FASCINATING FACT**...
> The USS *Monitor*, engineered by the Swedish-American John Ericsson, was the first American Union ironclad battleship. It took part in the first-ever battle between two ironclads. The vessel was described as a 'cheesebox on a raft', as it consisted of a huge iron turret and two cannons on an extremely flat deck.

◀ *During the first 20 years of his life, Alexander III had no prospect of succeeding to the Russian throne because he had an elder brother, Nicholas.*

1877 American inventor Thomas Alva Edison developed the phonograph. Known as one of the most successful inventors in history, Edison patented over 1000 inventions in his lifetime, including the electric light bulb.

1877 The American-based British photographer Eadweard Muybridge invented the zoopraxiscope, a forerunner of the movie projector.

1879 In eastern South Africa, British forces defeated the Zulus in the Zulu War and annexed Natal (now KwaZulu/Natal), a territory in South Africa.

1881 Alexander III became the tsar of Russia after his father, Alexander II, was assassinated. The reign of Alexander III was marked by economic reforms, but savage political repression.

1885 German engineer Karl Benz developed and commercialized the world's first car, the three-wheeled Benz car. He later joined forces with Daimler to form the automobile company which later became Mercedes-Benz.

151

1889 The British South Africa Company was granted a royal charter and given a vast stretch of land in south-central Africa. The company was established by the British imperialist Cecil Rhodes.

1889 The Brazilian monarchy was overthrown and the Republic of Brazil was founded.

1889 The Eiffel Tower was built in Paris for the World Exhibition, which was held to celebrate the 10th anniversary of the French Revolution. Built by Gustave Eiffel, the structure remained the tallest in the world until the Chrysler building was completed in 1930.

1891 A liberal government came to power in New Zealand, marking the beginning of a period of economic growth.

1893 The Independent Labour Party was founded in England as a representative body of the British working classes.

▲ *The Eiffel Tower is made of over 18,000 pieces of iron held together by two and a half million rivets. It took about 300 workers to erect the tower.*

1894–1895 Japan established itself as a major power when it defeated China in the Sino-Japanese War. The Treaty of Shimonoscki liberated Korea from China, while Japan was given Taiwan and the Liaotung Peninsula in Manchuria.

1895 The German physicist Wilhelm Conrad Röntgen took an x-ray of his wife's hand, the world's first x-ray of the human body. He was awarded the first Nobel Prize for Physics in 1901.

1896 The Italian physicist Guglielmo Marconi invented radio telegraphy. In 1909 he received the Nobel Prize for his pioneering work.

1897 German engineer Rudolf Diesel invented the world's first diesel engine and displayed it at the Paris World Fair.

...FASCINATING FACT...

In 1899, an Italian baker called Raffaele Esposito invented the classic pizza. When King Umberto and Queen Margherita visited Raffaele's restaurant, the baker decided to decorate his flattened bread with the colours of Italy. He added tomato, mozzarella cheese and basil as the topping to represent the red, white and green colours of the Italian flag. That is how the classic pizza came to be known as the Margherita pizza!

1898–1903

1898 The United States declared war against Spain in support of the Cuban struggle for independence, and defeated them in naval battles off the Philippines and Cuba. Spain agreed to give up its claim to Cuba.

1899–1902 British imperial forces defeated the Boer settlers of South Africa after a long, war. The war ended with the Treaty of Vereeniging, by which the Transvaal province and the Orange Free State became Britsh colonies.

1899–1961 American novelist Ernest Hemingway lived during this period. *A Farewell to Arms* is his most famous work. He was awarded the 1954 Nobel Prize for Literature.

1900 In China, the government-sponsored Boxer Rebellion against foreigners and Christians was put down when international forces captured Peking and forced the Ch'ing empress to flee.

1900 Vittorio Emanuele III ascended the Italian throne when his father Umberto I was assassinated.

1900 The independent Republic of Hawaii became a part of the United States.

1901 The Commonwealth of Australia Constitution Act was passed by the British Parliament, establishing the Commonwealth of Australia. The Act unified the colonies of New South Wales, Queensland, Tasmania, Victoria, South Australia and Western Australia.

1901 The Italian physicist Guglielmo Marconi received the first trans-Atlantic radio signal, sent from England to Newfoundland. The message was the Morse code for 'S'.

1902 French illusionist and filmmaker Georges Méliès produced *Le Voyage dans la lune* (A Trip to the Moon), a science-fiction story in 30 scenes. It was the first film of its kind and was also the first to be shown internationally.

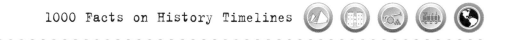

▲ *Marie Curie (left) and her daughter (right). Marie Curie was initially not allowed to attend universities in Russia and Poland because she was a woman.*

1903 French physicists Marie Curie, Pierre Curie and Henri Becquerel were awarded the Nobel Prize for Physics for their research on radioactivity.

1903–1950 British novelist George Orwell lived during this period. His greatest works are *Animal Farm* and *Nineteen Eighty-Four*. The author's pen name was George Orwell, while his real name was Eric Arthur Blair.

1903

January 10, 1903–May 20, 1975 The British sculptor Barbara Hepworth lived during this period. Her new and original style influenced many 20th-century artists.

April 1903 In the Russian province of Kishinev mobs attacked Jews, killing 45 and wounding more than 600. Nearly 1500 Jewish homes were looted.

May 29, 1903–July 27, 2003 The British-born US actor Bob Hope lived during this period. One of America's greatest entertainers, he performed for more than 80 years in a variety of roles as a comedian, singer, dancer and actor in vaudeville, on Broadway, in Hollywood, on radio and on television.

July 1–19, 1903 French cyclist and journalist Henri Desgrange organized the first Tour de France bicycle race. The event was so popular that it has been held every year since its inception.

July 11, 1903 King of Serbia Alexander I Obrenovich and his wife Queen Draga Mashin were killed by rebel army officers. The nobleman Peter Karageorgevich became king and followed a pro-Russian policy.

July 16, 1903 The American industrialist Henry Ford founded the Ford Motor Company. Henry Ford introduced the concept of assembly-line production of cars, which heralded a revolution in the automobile industry.

August 1903 The Russian Social-Democratic Workers' Party split into two groups – Bolsheviks and Mensheviks. At the Second Congress meeting of the party, its two leaders, Vladimir Lenin and Julius Martov, had an argument that led to the party being divided into two.

August 2, 1903 The Macedonians rose in protest for freedom from Ottoman rule with the Macedonian Ilinden Uprising, but the Ottoman Turks suppressed the uprising, killing hundreds of people and destroying nearly 20 villages.

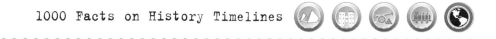

September 25, 1903–February 25, 1970 The American painter Mark Rothko lived during this period. Among the most significant artists of the 20th century, he pioneered the abstract expressionism style of painting. This style was marked by free and spontaneous expression of emotions.

October 28, 1903–April 10, 1966 The British novelist Evelyn Waugh lived during this period. Regarded as one of the most gifted satirical novelists of his time, *Brideshead Revisited* is considered to be his greatest novel.

◀ *Many Russian Jews moved to other countries, such as the United States, following violence against them in Russia.*

1903-1904

November 3, 1903 With the help of the United States, Panama separated from Colombia and became known as the Republic of Panama. The United States paid Colombia 25 million dollars in compensation so Panama could be recognized as independent.

November 18, 1903 The United States and Panama signed the Hay–Bunau-Varilla Treaty. It gave the United States exclusive rights to the Panama Canal and committed the United States to protect Panama in return.

December 17, 1903 The American inventors Wilbur Wright and Orville Wright invented the first powered flying machine. The Wright Brothers named their aeroplane the *Flyer*. The maiden flight of the Wright *Flyer*, at Kitty Hawk in North Carolina, lasted about 30 seconds.

1903 The first ever transcontinental trip by car was completed successfully, lasting 52 days between San Francisco and New York.

January 11, 1904 The Herero people of southwest Africa revolted against their German colonizers. The revolt was unsuccessful and over the next few years nearly 60,000 Hereros were killed.

February 8, 1904 The Russo-Japanese War broke out with a Japanese fleet making a surprise attack on the Russian navy at Port Arthur.

April 8, 1904 England and France began a period of friendly cooperation by signing the Entente Cordiale.

May 4, 1904 Sir Frederick Henry Royce of England manufactured the very first Royce car. The car, which was designed at Royce's Manchester factory, had two cylinders, a three-speed gearbox and an open, four-seat body.

▼ *Kitty Hawk, a town located in Dare County, North Carolina, became famous when the Wright Brothers made the first powered flight from a sand dune in the Kill Devil Hills.*

May 11, 1904–January 23, 1989 The Spanish artist Salvador Dalí lived during this period. He was one of the most significant artists of surrealism and soon became one of the greatest painters of the 20th century. Dalí's paintings were mainly a reflection of his dreams. Surrealism essentially drew on the subconscious mind and fantasies, uniting these with conscious reality.

. . . **FASCINATING FACT**. . .
Surrealism was created to break out of the regular and predictable forms of imagery used in art and literature. The artist or writer presents a very realistic image in a very unrealistic situation, which results in the image being startling and unexpected. One of the most famous images used in surrealistic paintings is Rene Margritte's mirror.

159

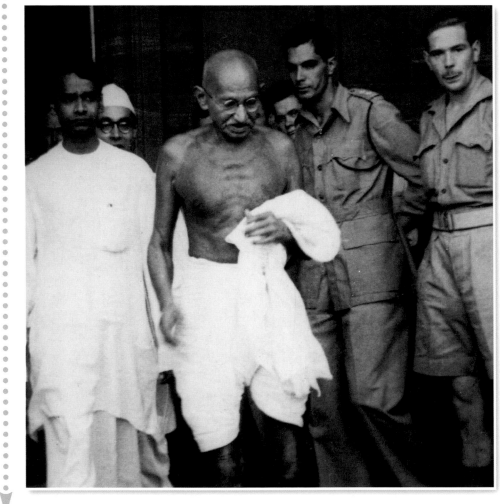

▲ *Mohandas Karamchand Gandhi was called 'Mahatma', which means 'great-souled'.*

January 22, 1905 The Russian police opened fire on workers participating in a peaceful march at St Petersburg, Russia. More than 100 people died in the massacre was followed by strikes in other cities, peasant uprisings and mutinies in the army. The uprising led to the establishment of an elected parliament, but the tsar kept real power for himself.

May 27–29, 1905 In the Russo-Japanese War, the Japanese fleet destroyed the Russian fleet in the Battle of Tsushima. The peace treaty recognized Japan's control over Korea and also gave Japan the Liaotung Peninsula, South Manchurian railroad and half of Sakhalin Island.

June 30, 1905 German physicist Albert Einstein published the *General Theories of Relativity*.

October 16, 1905 In India, British Viceroy Lord Curzon divided the province of Bengal in two. This caused discontent and accelerated the Indian nationalist movement.

October 30, 1905 Tsar Nicholas II issued the October Manifesto, ending the absolute power of the crown and promising to create a Constitution.

November 28, 1905 The Irish nationalist party Sinn Féin was founded. In the Irish language, Sinn Féin means 'ourselves'. The goal of the party is the independence of Ireland.

February, 1906 HMS *Dreadnought* was launched by the British Navy. It was the first modern battleship, powered by steam turbines and fitted with big guns.

September 1906 In South Africa, Mohandas Karamchand Gandhi led a protest against the Government order that all Asians had to be fingerprinted.

1907 British-Indian author and poet Rudyard Kipling was awarded the Nobel Prize for Literature. His most famous works are *Kim* and *The Jungle Book*.

1908–1910

1908 British army officer Robert Baden-Powell founded the Boy Scout movement. He wrote *Scouting for Boys* in the same year.

August 1908 The Chinese monarchy presented its proposal for gradually adopting constitutional rule in China.

October 6, 1908 Austria announced its decision to make Bosnia-Herzegovina a part of the Austria-Hungary Empire. This decision angered the natives of Bosnia-Herzegovina as well as Serbia and the Ottoman Turks.

October 10, 1908 The province of Bulgaria declared its independence from the Ottoman Empire. Bulgarian prince Ferdinand was made the first king.

October 10, 1908 The Belgian Parliament declared the Congo Free State in Africa a Belgian colony.

January 28, 1909 José Miguel Gómez was elected the president of Cuba.

February 12, 1909 The National Association for the Advancement of Colored People (NAACP) was founded in New York.

May 31, 1910 Transvaal, Cape Colony, Orange Free State and Natal joined together to form the Union of South Africa. The first elected prime minister of the new republic was Louis Botha.

August 27, 1910–September 5, 1997 Mother Teresa lived during this period. She founded the Missionaries of Charity in Calcutta, India. She dedicated her life to serving lepers and the poor. Mother Teresa recieved the Nobel Peace Prize in 1979 and was beatified (declared 'blessed' by the Pope) in 2003.

1910–1911 Portuguese revolt against the monarchy forced King Manuel II to flee. The Portuguese Republic was formed and Manuel José de Arriaga was elected its first president.

▶ Robert Baden-Powell's role in the siege of Mafeking during the South African War made him a national hero in Britain.

1912–1914

▲ *Archduke Francis Ferdinand and his wife Sophie, countess von Chotek, visited Sarajevo. Less than an hour after this photo was taken, they were both assassinated.*

February 1912 The Qing monarchy of China gave up their claim to the throne. The Chinese republic came into being.

April 14–15, 1912 The British luxury liner *Titanic* sank in the Atlantic on its maiden voyage to New York from Southampton, England. Over 1500 passengers and crew were killed in the tragic accident.

October 8, 1912 The Balkan League, comprising Greece, Serbia, Bulgaria and Montenegro, declared war on the Ottoman Empire to free Macedonia from Turkish rule. The Ottoman Turks lost the war.

1914 British comedian Charlie Chaplin began his career in Hollywood movies. He became famous for his baggy trousers, floppy shoes and little moustache.

April 2, 1914–August 5, 2000 British actor Sir Alec Guinness lived during this period. He won an Oscar for his role in *Bridge on the River Kwai*.

June 28, 1914 Archduke Francis Ferdinand, heir to the throne of Austria-Hungary, was killed at Sarajevo by a Serbian patriot.

July 28, 1914 The Austrian emperor Franz Joseph declared war against Serbia, starting World War I.

July 31, 1914 Russia joined the war to defend its ally, Serbia.

August 1, 1914 Germany declared war against Russia. Just two days after that it attacked France as well.

August 4, 1914 Germany invaded Belgium, a country allied to Britain. Britain declared war on Germany.

August 6, 1914 Austria-Hungary declared war against Russia. Later in the month, Japan declared war on Germany.

1914–1915

August 14, 1914 France and Germany fought the Battle of the Frontiers. This was a series of battles along the Franco-Belgian and Franco-German borders.

August 15, 1914 The Panama Canal was opened. Earlier, a French company had begun the construction of the canal, but the enterprise collapsed in 1889. In 1904, the United States was granted the Panama Canal Zone and construction began in 1904. The canal enabled the ships travelling between the Atlantic and Pacific oceans to avoid the circumnavigation of South America.

August 26–30, 1914 German forces crushed the Russian army in the Battle of Tannenberg.

▶ *William II was German emperor (kaiser) during World War I. After the war, he went into exile in the Netherlands.*

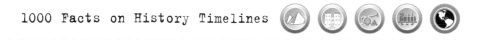
September 6–12, 1914 In the first Battle of the Marne, French forces halted the invading Germans and pushed them back with the help of British Expeditionary Forces.

October 29–30, 1914 Turkey allied with Germany and the Turkish fleet, led by the German warship *Goeben*, attacked several Russian ports, including Odessa.

November 1, 1914 Russia, France and Britain declared war against Turkey.

December 25, 1914 A temporary and unofficial truce was declared during Christmas among troops on the Western Front.

April 22, 1915 German troops used poison gas to attack Allied forces in the Second Battle of Ypres, introducing the concept of chemical warfare.

April 25, 1915 Allied forces began their campaign against Turkey by attacking Gallipoli near the Turkish capital of Constantinople.

May 17, 1915 British liner *Lusitania* was torpedoed by a German U-boat. Nearly 1200 passengers were killed, including 128 United States citizens.

...FASCINATING FACT...

Trench warfare was one of the most effective tactics used by the Germans in World War I. Three to four lines of long and deep trenches were dug at the battlefront, each with a protective barbed wire barrier. The trenches were cut in a zigzag fashion and were connected to one another through underground passages. They were large enough to accommodate first-aid stations, kitchens, toilets and ammunition stores.

1916-1917

February 21–December 18, 1916 France defeated Germany in the Battle of Verdun, one of the longest military encounters in World War I.

April 24, 1916 Irish republicans began the Easter Rebellion in Dublin. British troops suppressed the revolt swiftly and its leaders were executed.

May 31–June 1, 1916 British and German fleets engaged in the Battle of Jutland, held to be the greatest naval encounter in World War I. There was no clear winner. Germany destroyed more ships and men, but the British retained control of the North Sea.

▶ *Russian soldiers joined the people of St Petersburg (called Petrograd at that time) in the revolution that broke out in March 1917. The tsar was forced to step down.*

July 1–November 13, 1916 Britain introduced the battle tank for the first time in the Battle of the Somme, an Allied attack on German forces on the western front. The tanks could easily cross the muddy, uneven terrain, but suffered frequent mechanical failure.

August 28, 1916 Italy joined the war against Germany and Austria-Hungary.

March 15, 1917 Tsar Nicholas II was forced to give up his throne and a provisional government came to power in Russia. The new government introduced many democratic reforms, but decided to continue the war and rapidly lost popularity to a rival group called the Petrograd Soviet of Workers' and Soldiers' Deputies.

April 9, 1917 The United States joined the war on the Allied side.

June 27, 1917 Greece joined the Allied forces after pro-German king Constantine I abdicated in favour of his son Alexander I.

November 7, 1917 The Communists, led by Vladimir Iilych Lenin, established the Soviet Republic. In 1918, Lenin made peace with Germany. During the Russian Civil War that followed, he launched a campaign called 'Red Terror', aimed at eliminating political opponents.

...FASCINATING FACT...
After the first modern Olympic Games were held in April 1896, the tradition continued every four years, except in 1916, 1940 and 1944, due to the world wars. The Olympic flag, designed by the founder of the modern Olympics, Pierre de Coubertin, was first seen in 1920 at Antwerp. Coubertin also created the Olympic motto, Citius–Altius–Fortius ('Faster–higher–stronger') and the Olympic oath.

1917–1919

December 6, 1917 Finland declared its independence from Russia.

1918 Lithuania declared its independence from Russia and Germany.

1918 Tsar Nicholas II and his family were captured by communist troops at Tsarskoye Selo and taken to Siberia. Later, they were moved to Yekaterinburg in the Ural Mountains. In July, Tsar Nicholas II and his family were executed by Bolshevik gunmen.

August 8, 1918 German forces launched the Second Battle of the Somme to capture Amiens before proceeding to Paris. German troops led by General Erich Ludendorff forced the British to retreat to Amiens. Over 200,000 British soldiers were captured in the battle. The Germans suffered 300,000 casualties. A counterattack by British and French troops forced the Germans to turn back, producing an unlikely victory for the Allies.

September 27, 1918 Allied forces broke through the Hindenburg Line, a fortification that the Germans had successfully defended until then.

October 28, 1918 Czechoslovakia declared its independence from Austria-Hungary.

November 9, 1918 Kaiser Wilhelm II, Emperor of Germany, fled to Holland.

November 11, 1918 Peace was declared and World War I ended.

December 1, 1918 The kingdom of Serbs, Croats and Slovenes (later Yugoslavia) was formed. The Serbian Karadjordjevic dynasty ruled the new kingdom.

February 23, 1919 Journalist and ex-soldier Benito Mussolini founded the Italian Fascist Party.

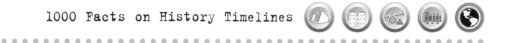
April 1919 In the Russo-Polish war, Poland successfully stood up against Russian attacks, with the help of France. The Treaty of Riga gave Poland parts of Belarus and Poland.

▶ *Tsar Nicholas II and his family.*

1919

May 1919 The Amir of Afghanistan, Amanullah Khan, led Afghani forces in the Third Anglo-Afghan War. Afghanistan won its independence from Britain.

May 18, 1919–February 21, 1991 The British ballerina Dame Margot Fonteyn lived during this period. She travelled all over the world performing a variety of roles in classics such as *Swan Lake*, *Sleeping Beauty* and *Ondine*.

May 25, 1919 Volcano Kloet erupted in Java, killing 16,000 people.

June 28, 1919 Germany and the Allied countries signed the Treaty of Versailles. As a result, Germany lost about 10 percent of its European territory and promised to pay the Allies to make reparation for war damage.

July 20, 1919 Edmund Hillary, explorer and mountaineer from New Zealand, was born. Hillary, along with Tenzing Norgay, became the first to reach the summit of the Mount Everest.

August 11, 1919 The Weimar Constitution was passed by the German Assembly and the new German Weimar Republic was established with Friedrich Ebert as its first president.

September 10, 1919 Austria and the Allied countries signed the Treaty of Saint-Germain, whereby Czechoslovakia, Hungary, Poland and the kingdom of Serbs, Croats and Slovenes gained their independence.

October 28, 1919 The United States Congress passed the National Prohibition Act (also called the Volstead Act), banning the manufacture and sale of liquor. The prohibition was removed in 1933.

November 27, 1919 Bulgaria was forced to sign the Treaty of Neuilly, giving away large portions of its territories to Yugoslavia and Greece. Bulgaria also had to reduce its army to just 20,000 soldiers and pay compensation to countries it had fought against.

172

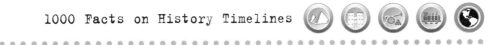
November 28, 1919 Nancy Astor became the first woman to be elected to the British House of Commons.

▲ *David Lloyd George, British prime minister (1916–1922) who guided his country through the latter part of World War I.*

1919–1921

December 24, 1919 Civil war broke out in Russia between the Red Army of the Communist government and the White Army of the anti-Communists. The Communists emerged victorious.

1919–1926 Spain fought the Rif War against the Rif and Jibala people of Morocco. The war ended with Spain's conquest of western Sahara.

January 2, 1920–April 6, 1992 Russian-born American author Isaac Asimov lived during this period. *Foundation*, *Foundation and Empire* and *Second Foundation* are some of his works.

August 10, 1920 Ottoman Turkey signed the Treaty of Sèvres. The treaty granted Armenia its independence and Greece won control over parts of Thrace (in the southeastern Balkans, Europe), Anatolia (in Turkey) and the Dardanelles (strait in northwestern Turkey).

December 1, 1920 General Álvaro Obregón was elected president of Mexico. Under his rule the civil war that had troubled Mexico since 1909 ended.

December 16, 1920 A major earthquake in the Gansu province of China killed nearly 200,000 people.

1920 In Germany, the German Workers' Party was renamed the National Socialist German Workers' (or Nazi) Party when Adolf Hitler became its leader.

1921 French bacteriologists Albert Calmette and Camille Guérin developed the BCG (Bacillus Calmette-Guérin) vaccination against tuberculosis.

1921 Albert Einstein was awarded the Nobel Prize for Physics.

1921–1924 Mongolia drove the Chinese from its territory with the help of Russian forces. The Mongolian People's Republic was founded.

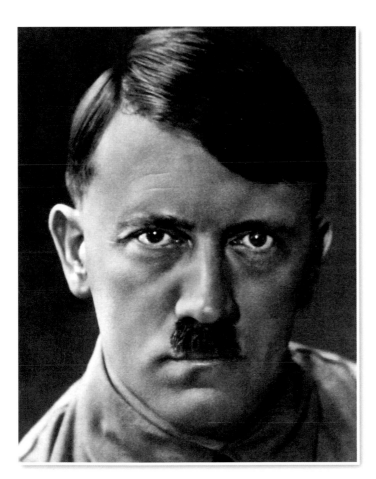

◄ *Adolf Hitler began his autobiography* Mein Kampf *in prison following his arrest in 1923.*

1921-1923

December 6, 1921 The Anglo-Irish Treaty was signed, which laid the foundation of the Irish Free State. The Northern Irish counties of Antrim, Armagh, Down, Fermanagh, Londonderry and Tyrone chose to remain under British rule.

January 1922 Micheal Collins, Irish Republican Army (IRA) leader, was made chairman of the provisional Irish government. Rebels opposed to the Anglo-Irish Treaty killed him on August 22.

February 2, 1922 *Ulysses*, an epic novel written by Irish author James Joyce, was published in Paris. It is considered one of the greatest literary classics of the 20th century.

June 10, 1922–June 22, 1969 American singer and actress Judy Garland lived during this period.

> ...FASCINATING FACT...
> British archaeologist Howard Carter is well known as the person who unearthed Pharaoh Tutankhamen's tomb. Before he made this famous discovery, he had discovered six other royal tombs, including those of Hatshepsut and Thuthmose IV. In 1907 Lord Carnarvon began sponsoring Carter's quest for Tutankhamen's tomb. By 1922 Carnarvon had lost hope of finding anything and had ordered Carter to return home after one last season. Carter discovered the tomb on his last attempt!

November 4, 1922 British archeologist Howard Carter discovered Pharaoh Tutankhamen's tomb in Thebes, Egypt.

December 6, 1922 The Irish Free State was established with William Thomas Cosgrave as its president and Timothy Michael Healy as its governor-general.

December 30, 1922 The Union of Soviet Socialist Republics (USSR) was founded. It comprised Russia, Ukraine, Belorussia and Transcaucasian Federation.

1923 The International Criminal Police Organization (Interpol) was established in Vienna, Austria.

1923 Spanish inventor Juan de la Cierva invented the autogiro, a low-cost alternative to the helicopter that proved of use for only small aircraft.

◄ *The Golden Mask of Pharaoh Tutankhamen can be seen at the Egyptian Museum in Cairo.*

1923-1928

October 29, 1923 Turkey became a republic and Sultan Abdul Mejid II was sent into exile. The new government, headed by Kemal Ataturk, defeated Greece and regained much lost territory.

November 8–9, 1923 In Germany, Adolf Hitler's Nazi Party led a rebellion called the Beer Hall Putsch against the Weimar Republic. They were unsuccessful and Hitler was arrested. Hitler used his time in prison to write the book *Mein Kampf* (My Struggle) that set out his political thoughts.

April 3, 1924–July 1, 2004 American actor Marlon Brando lived during this period. He performed memorable roles in classic films such as *A Streetcar named Desire* and the *The Godfather* series.

1925–1927 Benito Mussolini, prime minister of Italy, dissolved the Italian Parliament and became dictator of Italy.

1926 John Logie Baird of Scotland invented the first television transmitter, which was capable of showing crude, flickering images.

August 6, 1926 *The Jazz Singer* became the first talking motion picture. It was produced by Warner Brothers and directed by Alan Crosland.

May 20–21, 1927 American pilot Charles A Lindbergh made the first non-stop solo flight across the Atlantic, from New York to Paris, in his monoplane *Spirit of St Louis*.

November 12, 1927 The Soviet Communist Party expelled Leon Trotsky. Joseph Stalin gained undisputed control of the Soviet Union.

1928 Russian-born American inventor Vladimir Zworykin patented his design for a colour television.

December 5, 1928 The Chaco War between Paraguay and Bolivia began.

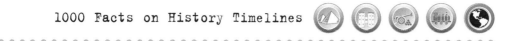

▲ *Joseph Stalin (right), seen here*
with Lenin (left), was one of the
most brutal dictators in history.

1929-1938

▲ *Edward VIII (second from left) became the only British monarch to resign voluntarily when he abdicated in order to marry Wallis Simpson.*

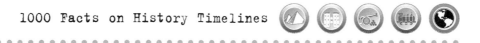

October 25, 1929 The New York Stock Market crashed. This marked the beginning of the Great Depression, a period of global economic crisis which lasted almost ten years.

March 9, 1932 The Japanese established the state of Manchukuo in Manchuria and appointed the last Qing emperor of China, P'u-yi, as head of the new state.

1933 Nearly 11,000 out of the 25,000 banks in the United States had to close down due to losses suffered during the Great Depression.

January 30, 1933 Adolf Hitler became chancellor of Germany. The following year he assumed the title of *Führer* (leader) of Germany, took dictatorial power over Germany and began a rapid buildup of military power.

January 8, 1935–August 16, 1977 American singer Elvis Presley lived during this period. He was one of America's greatest singing sensations between the mid-1950s and 1960s and was called the 'King of Rock and Roll'.

October 3, 1935 Benito Mussolini sent the Italian army to invade Ethiopia.

January 20, 1936 George V died and was succeeded by his son Edward VIII as king of the United Kingdom. Edward soon became embroiled in a scandal and constitutional crisis over his choice of Wallis Simpson, a divorced American, as his wife and queen. In December Edward VIII gave up his claim to the English throne and his brother George VI succeeded him.

July 17, 1936 Civil war broke out in Spain when the Nationalist Party revolted against the ruling Republican government. After a bloody war, in which more than 500,000 people lost their lives, Nationalist Francisco Franco and his troops established themselves in Madrid in March 1938.

September 29, 1938 Hitler's Germany, seized Czechoslovakia. Poland, France and Britain then began to prepare for war with Germany.

1939-1940

September 1, 1939 World War II began with the German invasion of Poland. Britain and France declared war on Germany.

October 5, 1939 The Polish Army was completely routed and Germany took control of Poland. Germany and the Soviet Union shared Polish territories.

November 30, 1939 The Soviet Union invaded Finland as Finland refused to let the Russians establish a naval base in its territory. At first the Finns drove back the much larger Soviet armies, but were later forced to surrender.

1940 Russian forces occupied Lithuania, Estonia and Latvia.

May 10, 1940 German forces made surprise attacks in the Low Countries (Belgium, The Netherlands and Luxembourg) and France. The Germans used a new form of warfare called blitzkrieg. They used tanks called panzers supported by aircraft to punch through enemy lines, and then advanced at high speed to disrupt enemy supply lines.

May 10, 1940 Winston Churchill succeeded Neville Chamberlain as the prime minister of Britain.

May 1940 Allied British forces were forced to pull out of France, Belgium and Norway by the invading Germans.

June 10, 1940 Italy declared war on France and Britain.

June 22, 1940 France surrendered. German troops occupied more than half of France, including northern and northeastern France. The rest of France that remained independent was ruled from the town of Vichy.

July–September, 1940 The Battle of Britain was fought between the Royal Air Force (RAF) and the German Luftwaffe. The RAF won the battle, forcing Hitler to abandon his plans to invade Britain.

◀ Winston Churchill was awarded the Nobel Prize for Literature in 1953 and was knighted in the same year.

1941-1944

▲ *The Japanese attack on the United States fleet at Pearl Harbor, Hawaii, hastened the entry of the United States into World War II. American casualties included over 180 aircraft and more than 5000 lives, from the military and the civilian.*

January 20, 1941 Exiled emperor Haile Selassie came back to power in Ethiopia after defeating Italian forces with the help of British troops.

April 6, 1941 German forces attacked and defeated Yugoslavia and Greece.

April, 1941 German Afrika Korps led by General Erwin Rommel expelled the British from Libya.

184

June 22, 1941 Germany invaded the Soviet Union. Other Axis Powers also declared war on the Soviet Union.

December 7, 1941 Japanese aircraft attacked Pearl Harbor in Hawaii. The United States reacted by declaring war on Japan.

December 11, 1941 Germany and Italy declared war against the United States.

February 14–15, 1942 Singapore was captured by Japanese forces and the British forces in Singapore surrendered.

May 1942 American forces in the Philippines were forced to surrender to the Japanese and the island country came under Japanese control.

June–November 1942 British forces, led by Field Marshal Bernard L Montgomery, defeated the German Afrika Korps at El-Alamein.

February 2, 1943 German forces suffered their first big defeat at Stalingrad, where the 6th Army was forced to surrender. This was the beginning of the downfall of Nazi power.

May 13, 1943 German and Italian forces in North Africa surrendered to the Allies.

June 6, 1944 Allied Forces landed on the Normandy coast in France on D-Day.

October 1944 United States forces regained control of the Philippines from the Japanese.

1944–1946

October 2, 1944 The Polish uprising in Warsaw was put down by the Germans and the city of Warsaw was completely destroyed.

April 12, 1945 Franklin D Roosevelt died and Harry S Truman became the 33rd president of the United States.

April 1945 Russian troops captured Berlin and the United States took Nürnberg. Nazi leader Adolf Hitler killed himself.

April 28, 1945 Italian dictator Benito Mussolini was arrested during an attempt to escape across the frontier, and executed.

May 7, 1945 Germany surrendered unconditionally to the Allied powers.

August 6, 1945 The United States decided to use the atomic bomb against Japan. The first atomic bomb was dropped on Hiroshima using a special B-29 bomber of the American Air Forces. Almost the entire city was flattened and around 100,000 people were killed. A memorial park containing a museum and monuments has since been built in dedication to the victims.

August 9, 1945 The Soviet Union invaded Manchuria. Within a few days they captured Emperor P'u-yi and conquered the country, taking over all stocks of food, gold and machinery.

August 14, 1945 Japan announced its surrender.

September 2, 1945 Communist leader Ho Chi Minh declared Vietnam's independence from France.

October 24, 1945 The United Nations was established.

June 2, 1946 King Umberto II of Italy was exiled and the people of Italy established a republic. Enrico de Nicola was named as the temporary president.

◀ *United States aircraft bombed Nagasaki three days after the atomic bombing of Hiroshima, destroying one-third of the city.*

1946-1952

September 1946 King George II of Greece came back to power when the Greeks voted for the return of monarchy. This led to civil war against communist forces in northern Greece.

August 15, 1947 India gained independence from Britain and the separate Muslim state of Pakistan was formed. The part in the northwest was called West Pakistan, and the part to the northeast of India was called East Pakistan.

February 2, 1948 The Republican government of Czechoslovakia was overthrown by the Czechoslovakian Communist Party backed by forces from Soviet Russia. Klement Gottwald was made head of the new Communist government.

April 4, 1949 Belgium, Italy, Canada, the Netherlands, Portugal, Denmark, Britain, France, Iceland, Norway, Luxembourg and the United States signed the North Atlantic Treaty, forming the North Atlantic Treaty Organization (NATO). It was a military alliance formed to counter the potential threat of Soviet invasion of Western Europe.

October 1, 1949 Mao Tse-tung, leader of the Communist party of China, proclaimed himself the chairman of the People's Republic of China. He is credited with implementing the programme of industrialization in the country, as well as for redistribution of land to the peasants.

June 25, 1950 Communist North Korea invaded South Korea, beginning the Korean War.

April 1952 Military rule was ended in Bolivia when the National Revolutionary Movement (MNR) came to power. Víctor Paz Estenssoro became the president of Bolivia.

July 26, 1953 Fidel Castro began his fight against the Cuban dictator Fulgencio Batista with an attack on the Moncada Military Barracks in Santiago de Cuba. The revolutionary movement is known as the 26th July Movement.

May 7, 1954 French forces were defeated by the Viet Minh in the Battle of Dien Bien Phu. The Geneva Accord temporarily divided the country into the northern Communist area and the southern non-Communist area.

October 31, 1954 The Algerian war for independence from French colonial rule began under the leadership of the National Liberation Front (FLN).

▶ *Following the establishment of People's Republic of China, Mao ordered the redistribution of land and the elimination of rural landlords.*

1956-1961

◀ *Fidel Castro was premier of Cuba from 1959 until 1976. He set up a one-party government to assume complete power.*

1956 The Republic of Sudan became independent of Britain. Morocco declared independence from French rule and France granted complete independence to Tunisia.

July 26, 1956 Egyptian president Gamal Abdel Nasser declared ownership of the Egyptian government over the Suez Canal. Outraged by this, Britain and France invaded Egypt, allied to Israel. International pressure forced Britain and France to withdraw.

October 1956 Hungarians revolted against Soviet rule, but the Russians suppressed the uprising.

March 25, 1957 West Germany, Italy, France, Belgium, Luxembourg and the Netherlands signed the Treaty of Rome, establishing the European Economic Community (EEC), later the European Union (EU).

October 4, 1957 The Soviet Union sent *Sputnik 1*, the first man-made satellite, into outer space.

January 1, 1959 In Cuba, rebel forces led by Fidel Castro overthrew Fulgencio Batista. Castro became head of the government. Castro improved health services and worked towards improving literacy among the Cuban public.

March 1959 Tibetans revolted against Chinese rule. The Dalai Lama and his followers fled to India. The Chinese crushed the revolt with much bloodshed. They closed down Tibetan monasteries and other cultural centres, and brought millions of Chinese workers to Tibet.

1960 The French colony of the Republic of the Congo was granted complete political independence along with Nigeria, Madagascar, Mali, French Congo, Chad and Mauritania.

April 12, 1961 Russian cosmonaut Yuri Gagarin became the first man to go into outer space. His spacecraft *Vostok 1* made an orbit of the Earth in 1 hour and 29 minutes.

August 12–13, 1961 The Berlin Wall was erected between Communist east Berlin and American-British-occupied West Berlin. Germany had been politically divided into East and West Germany in 1949.

▶ *The first human traveller to outer space, Yuri Gagarin was conferred with the title of 'Hero of the Soviet Union'.*

1961-1964

► *Marilyn Monroe, whose real name was Norma Jean Mortenson, was only 36 years old when she died.*

1961 Tanganyika became independent and Julius Nyerere became its first president. Goa, Diu and Daman joined India from Portuguese rule.

1962 The Central African countries of Burundi and Uganda gained independence from Belgium and Britain respectively. Burundi was ruled by the native Tutsi tribe and in Uganda a federal government was formed with Milton Obote as the head of state.

July 10, 1962 The first communications satellite *Telstar*, made by John Robinson Pierce of Bell Laboratories, USA, was launched into space.

August 5, 1962 Marilyn Monroe, one of the greatest cinematic icons of all time, was found dead in her house in California, the United States. It is widely believed that she died from an overdose of sleeping pills, but her death remains shrouded in controversy.

October 1962 United States President John F Kennedy discovered that the Soviet Union placed missiles in Cuba aimed at United States cities. Following a period of tense weeks during which war seemed very likely, Russia finally backed down.

August 28, 1963 In the United States, Martin Luther King Jr, delivered his famous 'I have a dream' speech supporting civil rights.

November 22, 1963 John F Kennedy was shot dead by Lee Harvey Oswald in Dallas. He was succeeded by Lyndon B Johnson as United States president.

December 12, 1963 Kenya declared independence from British rule and Jomo Kenyatta became the first prime minister of the new nation.

July 2, 1964 The United States Congress passed the Civil Rights Act to end discrimination based on race, colour and religion.

August 18, 1964 British pop band The Beatles gave their first performance at Hamburg, Germany. They had been performing since 1956 as the Quarry Men and later as the Silver Beetles.

October 16, 1964 China became the fifth country (after the USA, USSR, Britain and France) to successfully test an atomic bomb.

...FASCINATING FACT...

During the Great Depression, an unemployed salesman from Pennsylvania called Charles Darrow invented a game that involved buying, selling and renting real estate. It became very popular among his family and friends, and he was soon selling copies of the game to big stores. In 1935, Parker Brothers, an American toy manufacturer, bought the game from Darrow and Monopoly was born! Darrow became a millionaire and Monopoly is still one of the bestselling board games.

1964-1970

October 24, 1964 Zambia (also called Northern Rhodesia) became independent, breaking away from the British-controlled Central African Federation. Kenneth Kaunda, president of the United National Independence Party (UNIP), became the president of the new republic.

August 9, 1965 Singapore broke away from the Federation of Malaysia and became an independent state.

September 30, 1966 The Bechuanaland British Protectorate in southern Africa declared its independence. It renamed itself the Republic of Botswana.

April 21, 1967 Greek military officer Colonel Georgios Papadopoulos overthrew King Constantine.

June 5–10, 1967 Israeli forces invaded Sinai, the West Bank, Jerusalem and the Golan Heights in Syria to prevent Egyptian and Iraqi forces from attacking Israel. The Six-Day War ended with Israel's triumph.

December 3, 1967 South African surgeon Christiaan Barnard successfully conducted the first heart transplant operation.

...FASCINATING FACT...

The use of slang has existed for several years, especially among younger people. The youth of the 1960s too had their own slang. Many of them are words still in use today and many were so strange, one could never guess their meaning. For example, 'church key' was slang for a soda can opener; to 'ape' was to become extremely angry; to 'choose off' was to pick a fight; a 'drag' was a short car race; and a 'jelly roll' was a hairstyle!

1968 The British rock group Led Zeppelin was formed. They were among the most popular groups of the 1970s and played an important role in the development of heavy metal music.

April 4, 1968 American civil rights leader Dr Martin Luther King, Jr was shot dead by James Earl Ray at Memphis. The assassination resulted in riots in several cities across the United States.

May 10, 1968 Representatives of the United States and Vietnam met in Paris for peace talks.

July 20, 1969 American astronaut Neil Armstrong became the first person to land on the Moon.

1970 The Republic of Biafra's rebellion against the central government in Nigeria was ended when Biafra surrendered and joined Nigeria. About one million people died in the fighting and in the famine that followed.

▲ Formed in 1968, the rock group Led Zeppelin remained popular through the 1970s. The group broke up in 1980.

1970-1974

December 1970 The Awami League led by Mujibur Rahman won the Assembly elections in East Pakistan. The party sought independence from West Pakistan, which retained a greater share of political and economic power.

January 25, 1971 In Uganda, Idi Amin overthrew Milton Obote, the head of state, and declared himself president of Uganda. During his reign he forced all Asians to leave Uganda, tortured and murdered several Ugandans and supported the Palestinian war against Israel.

March 1972 Continuing violence between the Protestants and Catholics of Northern Ireland led to the British Parliament ending Home Rule and bringing Northern Ireland directly under British rule.

December 18–28, 1972 Hanoi, the capital of North Vietnam, was heavily bombed by United States forces even as peace talks were going on between the American representative Henry Kissinger and the Vietnamese representative Le Duc Tho at Paris.

January 27, 1973 Fighting ended in Vietnam and in March, United States troops returned home. The war had claimed the lives of over two million people, including 58,000 Americans.

September 11, 1973 The Chilean Socialist leader Salvadore Allende was killed and Augusto Pinochet set up a military government in Chile.

1974 The military government in Greece resigned and Constantine Karamanlis set up a democratic government, bringing back order and peace to the country.

April 25, 1974 The dictatorship in Portugal was ended by rebel army officers who had founded the Armed Forces Movement. Military rule was established with General António de Spínola as the new president of Portugal.

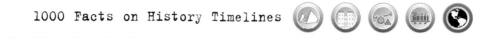

▲ *The United States Supreme Court voted unanimously in the Watergate trial and ordered President Nixon to hand over taped recordings related to the scandal. Chief Justice Burger presided over the trial, ultimately forcing Nixon to resign.*

July 15, 1974 Members of the Cypriot national guard overthrew Archbishop Makarios III, president of Cyprus. A few days later Turkish forces invaded Cyprus and occupied the northern part of the island.

July 24, 1974 The United States Supreme Court ordered President Richard Nixon to surrender White House tapes to special prosecutor Leon Jaworski, who was investigating the Watergate scandal. The controversy was related to the attempt to bug the headquarters of the Democratic National Committee at the Watergate complex in Washington, DC.

1974–1979

July 27–30, 1974 After the Watergate Scandal was revealed, President Nixon was charged with obstruction of justice, failure to follow the law and refusal to cooperate with the investigating authority. On August 8 he resigned.

April 1975 General Lon Nol, ruler of Cambodia, was overthrown. Khmer Rouge, a Communist organization, took control of the Cambodian government. Pol Pot, the Khmer leader, became prime minister.

▶ *Ruhollah Khomeini, recognized in his own time as one of the supreme religious leaders ('grand ayatollah') in Iran, steered the revolution against the ruling shah. Khomeini remained in absolute power for over a decade.*

198

April 1975 Bill Gates and Paul G Allen co-founded Microsoft Corporation, the leading developer of computer software in the world today.

August 1, 1975 Thirty-five European countries, the United States and Canada signed the Helsinki Accords. They recognized European borders established after World War II, agreed to uphold human rights and freedom, and promised to maintain friendly and cooperative relations with each other.

November 20, 1975 The Spanish dictator Francisco Franco died. Juan Carlos became king of Spain and introduced a democratic constitution.

July 2, 1976 North and South Vietnam were unified and named the Socialist Republic of Vietnam. The capital of the new nation was Hanoi, and the southern city of Saigon was renamed Ho Chi Minh City.

November 19–20, 1977 The Egyptian president, Anwar el-Sadat, made a historic visit to Israel. It marked the beginning of a peace process that ended the 30-year Egypt-Israel war.

February 5, 1979 The Grand Ayatollah, Seyyed Ruhollah Khomeini, led a revolution against the shah of Iran, overthrew the monarchy and established the Islamic Republic of Iran.

March 26, 1979 Anwar el-Sadat, president of Egypt, and Menachem Begin, prime minister of Israel, signed a peace treaty ending the war between the two nations.

April 1979 Rhodesia gained independence from the British and was renamed Zimbabwe.

1981-1990

▼ *The interior of St Paul's Cathedral combines elements of Neoclassical, Gothic and Baroque architecture.*

July 29, 1981 Charles, Prince of Wales, and Lady Diana Spencer were married at St Paul's Cathedral in London.

April 2, 1982 Argentina invaded the British controlled Falkland Islands and took control of Port Stanley, South Georgia and the South Sandwich islands. In June, Argentina surrendered the Falkland Islands to Britain after being defeated in battles fought on both land and sea.

1983 The first modern cellular telephone system, called the advanced mobile phone system (AMPS), developed by AT&T and Motorola, was introduced.

March 10, 1985 Mikahil Gorbachev was elected the general secretary of the Communist Party of the Soviet Union. His programmes of modernizing the Soviet economy and giving more independence to communist states that were part of the Soviet Union led to the breakup of the USSR.

November 1985 Microsoft Corporation introduced the Windows Operating System to its computer software.

April 25–26, 1986 An accident at the nuclear power plant at Chernobyl, Ukraine, killed 32 people. Several thousand people and animals were affected by the radiation.

1989 British scientist Tim Berners-Lee invented the World Wide Web.

1989 *Exxon Valdez*, one of the largest oil carriers ever built, ran aground off Alaska, and spilt 11 million gallons of oil, one of the worst oil spills in history.

November 9, 1989 The Berlin Wall was brought down. Communist governments across Eastern Europe gave way to democracy.

February 11, 1990 Nelson Mandela, the leader of the African National Congress, was released from prison after 26 years. His long struggle against discrimination ended apartheid in South Africa.

1990-1996

March 21, 1990 Namibia gained independence from South Africa. In 1989, elections were held in Namibia under the supervision of the United Nations (UN). Sam Nujoma, leader of the victorious South West Africa People's Organization (SWAPO), became president.

August 2, 1990 Iraqi forces made a surprise attack on Kuwait, starting the Persian Gulf War. The United States, NATO and Arab forces from several countries came together to free Kuwait from Saddam Hussein and his army. This was achieved in February 1991.

October 3, 1990 East and West Germany were reunified. Helmut Kohl became the first chancellor of the unified nation.

November 1991 Chechnya declared its independence from the USSR and established itself as a republic under the leadership of Dzhozkhar Dudayev.

December 25, 1991 Mikhail Gorbachev resigned from the post of president of the Soviet Union. By this time all the 15 communist countries that were once part of the USSR had declared their independence and 11 of these had formed the Commonwealth of Independent States (CIS).

...FASCINATING FACT...
The 50-km-long Channel Tunnel between England and France opened on May 6, 1994, allowing people to travel between the two countries in just 35 minutes. Built over a period of seven years, it took about 15,000 workers to construct this rail tunnel. The first passengers travelled on November 13, 1994.

April 7, 1992 Serbian forces began to attack the Bosnian capital Sarajevo and took control of the eastern part of Bosnia. In the next two years, hundreds of Bosnians were killed and thousands were forced to flee.

January 1, 1993 Czechoslovakia was split into the Czech Republic and Slovakia.

May 10, 1994 Nelson Mandela became the president of the Republic of South Africa.

January 20, 1996 Yasir Arafat was elected president of the Palestinian Authority, ruling Palestinian areas of the Gaza Strip and West Bank.

▶ *South African statesman Nelson Mandela.*

203

1997-2002

▲ *Fifty years of Queen Elizabeth II's reign in 2002 was marked by celebrations that included concerts, fireworks and a ritual march to St Paul's Cathedral.*

July 1, 1997 Hong Kong was handed over to China by Britain. It was made a special administrative region under the control of the Chinese government.

August 31, 1997 Diana, Princess of Wales (and former wife of Charles, Prince of Wales), was killed in an automobile accident in Paris.

May 12, 2000 President Kim Jong II of North Korea and President Kim Dae-jung of South Korea met in Pyongyang, North Korea. They agreed to end the state of war that had existed between the two nations since 1950.

June 10, 2000 Syrian president Hafez al-Assad died, and his son Bashar Assad succeeded him.

2001 The Islamic organization the Taliban controlled most parts of Afghanistan. It began by taking control of Kandahar in 1994 and then other parts of the country.

September 11, 2001 The twin towers of the World Trade Center in New York were hit by passenger aircraft hijacked by Al Qaeda militants. A short while later, the Pentagon in Washington was also similarly attacked. More than 3000 people were killed in these horrific incidents.

December 22, 2001 The Taliban was defeated and driven out of Kandahar, the Afghani capital. A temporary government was established with Hamid Karzai as the new leader of Afghanistan.

January, 2002 Euro coins and notes were introduced in 12 countries of the European Union.

June 3, 2002 A 'Party in the Palace' was organized at Buckingham Palace as part of British queen, Elizabeth II's, Golden Jubilee celebrations.

2003–2004

March 12, 2003 The Serbian Prime Minister Zoran Djindjic was assassinated in Belgrade.

April 4, 2003 American troops and tanks entered Baghdad, the capital of Iraq, and captured the airport. Hundreds of Iraqis fled the city. The next day, American and Kurdish forces jointly captured the Iraqi town of Mosul.

May 1, 2003 American President George W Bush announced the end of all major military operations against Iraq.

December 14, 2003 American troops captured Iraqi dictator Saddam Hussein at Tikrit, Iraq.

January 4, 2004 *Spirit*, the six-wheeled robot made by the United States space agency NASA, landed on Mars.

March 2, 2004 A group of terrorist suicide bombers killed 100 people and wounded 300 in the holy Muslim city of Karbala, and killed 58 people and wounded 200 others at Baghdad in simultaneous attacks at both places.

March 11, 2004 Three trains were blasted simultaneously in Madrid during the morning rush hour, killing nearly 200 and wounding more than 1400 people. Islamic militants were believed to have been responsible. As a result, the Spanish public elected a new government and withdrew its support for the war in Iraq.

May 9, 2004 Chechen President Akhmad Kadyrov was killed in a bomb blast along with five others while attending Victory Day celebrations at Chechnya's capital Grozny.

June 27, 2004 The American administration of Iraq ended and the governance of the country was given back to the Iraqis.

August 11, 2004 American marines, helicopters and tanks launched a heavy attack on the Iraqi holy town of Najaf.

December 26, 2004 A massive earthquake under the sea off Sumatra triggered massive tsunami waves across the Indian Ocean, killing over 100,000 people. The UN stepped in with humanitarian aid.

▼ *The United Nations flag carries the official emblem of the organization in white against a blue backdrop. The emblem is a circular world map, as projected from the North Pole, enclosed within olive branches – a symbol for peace.*

Index

B

Index

Index

Index

Index

Index

Index

Index

Acknowledgements

All artworks are from Miles Kelly Artwork Bank

The Publishers would like to thank the following picture source
whose photograph appears in this book:

p98 Macduff Everton/CORBIS, p101 Farrell Grehan/CORBIS,
p195 Pictoral Press.com

All other photographs from:

Castrol, CMCD, Corbis, Corel, digitalSTOCK, digitalvision
Flat Earth, Hemera, ILN, John Foxx, PhotoAlto, PhotoDisc
PhotoEssentials, PhotoPro, Stockbyte